JI/SRI LA   Replacement for lost copy '   HC
424
.LAL

WITHDRAWN

Social Science Library
Oxford University Library Services
Manor Road
Oxford OX1 3UQ

29 AUG 1989

D0785968

Oxford University
Mansell Street,
Oxford OX1 3UC

WITHDRAWN

Impediments to Trade Liberalization in Sri Lanka

This is the sixth title, in the Thames Essay series, arising out of the Trade Policy Research Centre's programme of studies on the Participation of Developing Countries in the International Trading System, supervised by Martin Wolf as the Centre's Director of Studies. Earlier titles were

Myths and Reality of External Constraints on Development
by James Riedel

Economic Impact of Generalized Tariff Preferences
by Rolf J. Langhammer and André Sapir

East African Lessons on Economic Liberalization
by David Bevan, Arne Bigsten, Paul Collier and Jan Willem Gunning

Developing Countries in the GATT Legal System
by Robert E. Hudec

Impediments to Trade Liberalization in the Philippines
by Romeo M. Bautista

Other titles in the programme to be published as Thames Essays are provisionally entitled

Impediments to Trade Liberalization in Latin America
edited by Larry A. Sjaastad

Impediments to Trade Liberalization in the Republic of Korea
by Soogil Young

The cartoon by Kal on the cover appeared in *The Economist*, London, on 14 July 1984. In this Thames Essay on the efforts in the 1980s to liberalize the economy of Sri Lanka, under the Government of President Junius Jayawardena, the authors argue that after initial success the programme foundered because of the government's failure to stabilize the economy, leaving an unfinished agenda and leading to a partial reversal of the liberalization.

Thames Essay No. 51

Impediments to Trade Liberalization in Sri Lanka

BY

Deepak Lal

AND

Sarath Rajapatirana

Gower

Aldershot · Brookfield USA · Hong Kong · Singapore · Sydney

─────────── ◊ ───────────

for the
TRADE POLICY RESEARCH CENTRE
London

Copyright © 1989 by
TRADE POLICY RESEARCH CENTRE
1 Gough Square
London EC4A 3DE

062144

All rights reserved. No part of this publication may be reproduced, stored in a retrieval system, or transmitted in any form or by any means, electronic, mechanical, photocopying, recording or otherwise without the prior permission of Gower Publishing Company Limited.

First published 1989 by

Gower Publishing Company Limited
Gower House, Croft Road, Aldershot, Hampshire GU11 3HR
United Kingdom

Gower Publishing Company
Old Post Road, Brookfield, Vermont 05036
United States of America

Gower Publishing Australia
10 George Place, Artamon, New South Wales 2064,
Australia

ISSN 0306 6991
ISBN 0 566 05340 3

British Library Cataloguing-in-Publication Data
Lal, Deepak.
    Impediments to Trade Liberalization in Sri Lanka.
    (Thames Essay No. 51)
    1. Sri Lanka — Commerce
    I. Title II. Rajapatirana, Sarath
    382'.09549'3   HF 3770.8.25

Library of Congress Cataloging-in-Publication Data
Lal, Deepak.
    Impediments to Trade Liberalization in Sri Lanka.
    (Thames Essay No. 51)
    Bibliography: p.56
    I. Rajapatirana, Sarath.   II. Title.
    III. Series.
HF1586.8.L35   1987   382'.3'095493

Printed and Bound by Athenæum Press
Newcastle upon Tyne

HF 1586.8 LAL

Contents

List of Tables

Biographical Notes

DEEPAK LAL has been Professor of Political Economy at University College, University of London, since 1984, where he has taught since 1970. In 1983-87, he was on leave of absence at the World Bank, in Washington, serving as Research Administrator between 1984 and 1987.

Professor Lal was a member of the Indian Foreign Service in 1963-66. He then taught economics at Christ Church, University of Oxford, and was afterwards a Research Fellow at Nuffield College, also at Oxford. Professor Lal has served as a consultant to the Indian Planning Commission and the Ministries of Finance in South Korea, Sri Lanka and Jamaica.

The author of numerous articles in professional journals on issues of economic development and economic policy, Professor Lal's books include *Appraising Foreign Investment in Developing Countries* (1975), *Unemployment and Wage Inflation in Industrial Economies* (1977), *Men or Machines* (1978), *Prices for Planning* (1980), *Resurrection of the Pauper-labour Argument* (1981) and *The Poverty of 'Development Economics'* (1983).

SARATH RAJAPATIRANA is a Senior Economist at the World Bank, Washington, which he joined in 1975 as an Economic Adviser. He is the director of the World Bank's research programme on the comparative macro-economic performance of developing countries, having been staff director of the *World Development Report 1987*, and he is a member of the editorial board of the *World Bank Economic Review*.

After graduating from the University of Ceylon in 1964, he was a Fulbright Scholar at the University of Minnesota (1968-69), where he was subsequently awarded a fellowship. He returned to Sri Lanka to become Chief of Money and Banking Research at the Central Bank of Ceylon and also taught at the University of Ceylon and at the Bankers Training Insitute in Colombo.

On joining the World Bank, Dr Rajapatirana was a Country Economist on Burma and Nepal, in the South Asia Department, and later was a Senior Economist in the East Asia Department. In 1983-87 he was Chief of the Policy Analysis Unit in the Office of the Vice President of Economics and Research.

Preface

RELATIONS between developed and developing countries in the international trading system, whose norms, rules and procedures are set out in the General Agreement on Tariffs and Trade (GATT), have been reaching an *impasse*. For a quarter of a century, the developed countries have been allowing, or encouraging, the developing countries to become contracting parties to the GATT without requiring them to abide by the more important obligations of membership. What is more, they have acquiesced in the formal derogation from the principle of non-discrimination, which is the keystone of the GATT, to permit the Generalized System of Preferences (GSP) in favour of developing countries to be established and maintained.

At the same time, developing countries — especially the more advanced ones — have been faced with discriminatory protection against them whenever their exports have been uncomfortably successful in the markets of developed countries, such protection often taking the form of export-restraint arrangements negotiated 'outside' the framework of GATT norms, rules and procedures. Export restraints have become a major issue on the GATT agenda.

The costs to developing countries of limitations on their access to the markets of developed countries are not so much offset as multiplied by their more or less complete freedom to establish and maintain trade regimes which are highly protectionist and Byzantine in their complexity.

By the early 1980s, it was clear that the role of developing countries in the international trading system was bound to attract increasing attention, especially if a new 'round' of multilateral trade negotiations under GATT auspices was to be undertaken. Accordingly, the Trade Policy Research Centre, with the help of a grant from the Leverhulme Trust in London, embarked in 1983 on a major programme of studies on the Participation of Developing Countries in the International Trading System, supervised by Martin Wolf, at that time the Centre's Director of Studies. In the Uruguay Round negotiations, eventually launched at Punta del Este in Uruguay in September 1986, more is expected of developing countries and, indeed, developing countries are participating much more than they did in the previous Tokyo Round negotiations of 1973-79.

The purpose of the programme has been to clarify, for public discussion and policy formation, the underlying reasons for the current difficulties in relations between developed and developing countries in the GATT system. The programme focusses both on economic and legal issues in the GATT system *per se* and on impediments to trade liberalization in individual developing countries. The emphasis on the latter derived from the perception that the GATT framework of norms, rules and procedures can be no more than the 'handmaiden' of trade liberalization. Liberalization will not be brought about unless there is a consensus in the countries concerned on both its feasibility and its value in promoting their economic growth and development. The domestic impediments to trade liberalization have to be understood if they are to be overcome.

It is true for all countries that multilateral negotiations are a means more of achieving the trade liberalization that is already widely understood to be in each country's own interests than of liberalizing when no such benefit is seen. In other words, reciprocal bargaining is a way of overcoming domestic resistance to the trade liberalization that is strongly desired by important forces in each country, both in government and in society at large. A desire to liberalize, almost irrespective of what happens elsewhere, is particularly significant in small countries. The smaller the country, the less effective is its international bargaining power and, therefore, the less persuasive is the argument that improved access to markets abroad depends on the liberalization of access to its own market. For this reason, smaller countries usually liberalize only if there is a strong domestic consensus that such liberalization is in their own interests, such a consensus having been long established in countries like Sweden, Switzerland and Singapore.

From a trade-policy point of view, almost all developing countries are small. Thus the use they can or will make of the international trading system depends, in the first place, on the strength of the domestic desire to liberalize and, in the second place, on the role that international bargaining can play in the process. It is with these questions in mind that a number of country studies have been undertaken as part of the Centre's programme. Apart from the study of Sri Lanka reported in these pages, there are studies of Kenya and Tanzania in East Africa, of the Republic of Korea and the Philippines in East Asia and of Argentina, Brazil and Colombia in Latin America, listed at the front.

Deepak Lal, of University College, University of London, and Sarath Rajapatirana, a Senior Economist at the World Bank, find in the case of Sri Lanka an important example of the problems of liberalizing trade in a country with a long history of inward-looking policy. Particularly important in the case of Sri Lanka have been problems of macro-economic stabilization, which has proved, time and again, to be the most significant obstacle to successful liberalization.

At the time of independence in 1948, Sri Lanka was an open economy, which had a high standard of living relative to other Asian countries. But in the post-World War II period Sri Lanka fell far behind many other Asian developing countries. Furthermore, by the 1970s, the slow growth of the economy and the rapid growth of welfare entitlements were together generating an unsustainable fiscal position. The government of President Jayawardena, which came to power in 1977, was pledged to liberalize the economy, especially trade, and prune back the activities of the state.

Despite substantial initial successes, the programme as a whole has foundered, as the authors show, in ways all too familiar to students of liberalization attempts in the Southern Cone of Latin America: large fiscal deficits combined with substantial capital inflows generated a massive real appreciation of the rate of exchange (in this case via inflation); the external economic environment, especially the terms of trade, deteriorated sharply after 1979; and, in the face of these adverse shocks, there was a partial reversal of the liberalization itself. The study indicates how difficult it is to liberalize an economy suffering from a combination of serious fiscal imbalances and extensive trade-policy distortions. The problem can be exacerbated by large capital inflows, which have to be managed with great care.

Earlier drafts of the papers arising from the Centre's programme of studies were presented at a three-day research meeting in October 1984 at Wiston House, near Steyning, in the United Kingdom, attended by those engaged on the programme and a number of other scholars and officials. The meeting was immediately preceded by a two-day meeting, also at Wiston House, of a study group which is drawing together the conclusions of the programme of studies. This meeting, too, was attended by a number of officials. The two international meetings were funded by a grant from the Ford Foundation in New York while, as already mentioned, the programme of studies as a whole has been funded by the Leverhulme Trust in London.

The authors have been grateful for the comments of Paul Collier and Larry Sjaastad who were the discussants on their first draft at the Wiston House research meeting.

As usual, it has to be stressed that the views expressed in this Thames Essay do not necessarily represent those of members of the Council or those of the staff and associates of the Trade Policy Research Centre which, having general terms of reference, does not represent a consensus of opinion on any particular issue. The purpose of the Centre is to promote independent analysis and public discussion of international economic policy issues.

HUGH CORBET
Director
Trade Policy Research Centre

London
October 1988

Introduction

Martin Wolf

THE purpose of the programme of studies, of which this study is a part, has been to examine the obstacles to the increased participation of developing countries in the international trading system, as governed by the General Agreement on Tariffs and Trade (GATT). From the beginning, however, it was obvious that the principal obstacle to such participation was the inability and, indeed, the unwillingness of the countries concerned to contemplate a significant reduction in their own trade barriers. For this reason, a major part of the programme has been an examination of obstacles to trade liberalization, both political and economic, in a selected group of developing countries.

The countries included in the programme were Argentina, Brazil and Colombia in Latin America; the Republic of Korea, Sri Lanka and the Philippines in Asia; and Kenya and Tanzania in East Africa. In addition, in 1985 the Trade Policy Research Centre published a study, by T.G. Congdon, of the liberalization experience of countries in the Southern Cone of Latin America, focussing on the interesting and important experience of Chile, a study which is complementary to those appearing in the present programme.[1]

PURPOSE OF THE COUNTRY STUDIES

Since the starting point for the programme of studies was the fuller participation of developing countries in the international trading system, as regulated by the GATT, the group of countries selected for study may appear somewhat puzzling. There is very little concern within the GATT system about the policies of relatively small and poor developing countries like Kenya, Tanzania or Sri Lanka. Nobody expects even larger countries like Argentina, Colombia and the Philippines to make significant changes in their policies in the context of multilateral negotiations such as the Uruguay Round. Indeed, of the countries selected for study, only Brazil and the Republic of Korea are undoubtedly high on the list of those expected by the developed countries to participate more fully in the GATT system or, as it is sometimes put more controversially, to 'graduate'.

There are two major implications of this lack of interest in the policies of most of the countries under analysis. First, one might wish to argue that participation in the GATT can be the 'handmaiden' of trade liberalization by developing countries, as it has certainly proved to be in the case of the developed countries. More precisely, reciprocal bargaining could be a way of overcoming domestic resistance to trade liberalization, while international obligations could also be a bulwark against subsequent increases in protection. But such a justification for fuller participation in the GATT has only modest force, at best, in the case of most developing countries. One can hardly justify liberalization (or resistance to increases in protection) by reference to international repercussions if the reaction of the international community is going to be yawning indifference. Secondly, as a corollary of this very indifference, developing countries can, individually at least, have little impact on the obligations assumed or actions undertaken by other contracting parties of the GATT (including other developing countries).[2]

The reciprocal bargaining that is at the heart of the process of trade liberalization in the GATT framework is, by its nature, a game played by countries that have something with which to bargain. Small countries must, willy nilly, accept whatever crumbs fall from the negotiators' table. This does not mean, however, that negotiations in the GATT are of little importance for those countries. A world of stable, liberal and non-discriminatory trade policies is probably still more important for small, weak and trade-dependent economies than for the greater powers. It is just that the former can do little to bring it about.

What individual developing countries can do is position themselves to exploit the opportunies that will, one hopes, arise. But to achieve this goal they must first liberalize their trade policies. This, then, is the most important reason for examining impediments to trade liberalization in a number of developing countries.

Furthermore, trade liberalization by a number of developing countries would have an impact on the GATT system, even if undertaken outside that forum, provided it is associated with a rapid growth of their trade. The growth of exports (and imports) from Hong Kong, Singapore, the Republic of Korea and Taiwan shows that initially small economies can quite swiftly become important to the world economy. In fact, in 1984 the combined gross merchandise imports of these four trade-oriented developing economies was $109 billion, greater than those of Italy, France or the United Kingdom and seven times as much as those of either India or Brazil. (Indeed, *each* of the four imported far more than either of these latter countries.) In 1970, by contrast, the gross merchandise imports of the four developing economies had been less than $9 billion, almost exactly the same as those of Belgium at that time and about 40 per cent of those of the United Kingdom. Thus, the growth of the 'four little tigers', as they have sometimes been called, has been an important source of growth for world trade as a whole.[3]

Furthermore, successful trade liberalization by a large number of developing countries might lead to a change in the collective demands of developing countries. Up to now one of the most important goals of the developing countries has been that they remain free from most of the obligations of GATT membership and be allowed to pursue whatever protectionist trade policies they think appropriate. With widespread and successful liberalization, however, the demand could change and that, in turn, could make an important contribution to the viability of the system as a whole. In particular, developed countries might then feel somewhat less than they do now that liberalization is a cost borne by the rich for the benefit of the poor.

At the same time, membership of the GATT can offer some assistance to developing countries, when trying to liberalize. At present, the International Monetary Fund (IMF) and the World Bank are the main international institutions involved in helping developing countries with trade liberalization. In the case of the countries of Southern Europe, agreements with the European Community play a major role in assisting liberalization. But Mexico's accession to the GATT in 1986 indicates that membership can assist liberalization by signalling the commitment to liberalize and making that commitment more credible.[4]

Furthermore, even if one were mainly concerned with the prospects for trade liberalization by countries now expected to participate more fully in the GATT system, one could not focus only on those cases, since they represent too limited a sample. Lessons have to be drawn from a wider sample.

Last but not least, the aim of participation in the GATT is trade liberalization. From this perspective, it does not matter whether liberalization is achieved unilaterally or multilaterally. What matters is that it happens. It is necessary, therefore, to discover when and how liberalization is achieved.

CASE OF SRI LANKA

The study by Deepak Lal and Sarath Rajapatirana finds the case of Sri Lanka to be exemplary, because there has been an important attempt to reverse a long-standing policy of protection. But the attempt to reverse these policies has not gone smoothly. Particularly important in the case of Sri Lanka have been problems of macro-economic stabilization, which has proved time and again to be the most significant obstacle to successful trade liberalization.

At the time of independence in 1948 Sri Lanka was an open economy which had a high standard of living relative to other Asian countries. To give an indication, in 1960 per capita income in Sri Lanka was as high as in the Republic of Korea. But in the period after World War II Sri Lanka fell far behind many other Asian developing countries. Particularly significant was her poor export performance as the economy became increasingly protected.

Sri Lanka's economic problems can be related to two commitments: one to large social expenditures (from the 1930s) and the other to *dirigisme*, including extensive public ownership of industry (from the mid-1950s). Moreover, as has been the case in a number of other countries, the central instruments of *dirigisme* have been exchange and trade controls, which were introduced in 1960 and 1961 to tackle a deteriorating balance of payments position.

By the 1970s, the slow growth of the economy and the rapid growth of welfare entitlements were, together, generating an unsustainable fiscal position. Consequently, the government of President J.R. Jayawardena's United National Party (UNP), which came into power in 1977, was pledged to liberalize the economy, especially trade controls (but also controls over prices of goods and markets for labour and capital) and, in addition, to prune back the activities of the state.

The initial liberalization effort was impressive. It included a substantial devaluation, loosening of the system of exchange controls and quantitative restrictions on imports, removal of almost all price controls, adoption of measures to attract foreign private investment and a decision to raise nominal interest rates. Nevertheless, there remained a substantial unfinished agenda, including a need to reduce the variance in protection, to maintain a competitive real rate of exchange, to liberalize the domestic capital market and to increase the flexibility of the labour market. As the authors note, 'the aftermath of the liberalization can be analyzed in terms of the unfinished agenda'.

While performance following the reform package was greatly improved, there were worrying developments. Most important, perhaps, was the commitment by the government to three major public investment projects. Finance of these projects put substantial pressure on public finances. The budget deficit, far from being contained, was 20 per cent of GDP by 1980 and, at the same time, the current-account deficit in the balance of payments rose from 5.5 per cent of GDP in 1977 to 20 per cent in 1980. Meanwhile, the world environment was deteriorating rapidly following the second oil shock, combined with the 'Volcker shock' aimed at lowering global inflation. Sri Lanka's terms of trade fell by no less than 44 per cent between 1977 and 1982.

With the growing external imbalance caused by the public-sector deficit and the deteriorating external environment, the liberalization itself came under pressure. This reversal had the following main elements:

(a) Appreciation of the real exchange rate to absorb the capital inflow required to finance the fiscal deficit.

(b) Changes in import duties that tended to widen the variance in the effective rate of protection.

(c) Increased reliance on discretionary non-price incentives to promote exports.

(d) Continued distortions in the price of credit, which interacted with the trade regime to create differential incentives for exports and imports.

In short, despite the considerable successes associated with the liberalization programme, especially much faster economic growth, the agenda remains unfinished and, indeed, has been getting longer.

MAIN CAUSES OF PARTIAL REVERSAL

The very partial success of the attempt to reverse the errors of decades brings important lessons, lessons that have also emerged from experience with other such attempts.

In the first place, as the authors remark 'whilst the economy was being partly liberalized it was not stabilized'. The UNP

government inherited macro-economic imbalances characterized
by both a fiscal crisis and a chronic balance-of-payments
problem suppressed through tight exchange and import
controls. Unfortunately, the need to finance the big investment
projects created a new imbalance. Initially, Sri Lanka's
improved creditworthiness made it easy to finance that
imbalance by foreign borrowing, with capital inflows rising
from 5 per cent of GDP in the early 1970s to over 17 per
cent in 1981. These capital inflows created what has come,
in other contexts, to be called a 'Dutch disease' problem.[5]

In the second place, although capital inflows must necessarily
be associated with an appreciation of the real rate of exchange,
in the case of Sri Lanka that appreciation was unfortunately
brought about by inflation. This effect could easily have been
avoided by appreciation of the nominal exchange rate or
reductions in taxes on imports. Furthermore, it is questionable
whether the inflows were even desirable or, in other words,
whether the return on the investments is likely to prove
adequate to service the debt when the inflows themselves fall
back to levels that are more sustainable in the long term.

In the third place, there are questions about the timing and
sequencing of the liberalization. The timing was unfortunate
because of the condition of the world economy. Sri Lanka,
like other economies that started to liberalize in the 1970s after
missing the opportunities of the 1950s and 1960s, has suffered
the consequence of a profound misjudgment.

The sequencing, however, does raise additional issues. The
authors note that the decision to reform trade policy gradually
may have been an error because it allowed the formation of
strong lobbies against completion of the reform. Also important
is the question of the appropriate timing of the liberalization
of capital markets and of the capital account of the balance
of payments, as against the liberalization of the market for
goods.[6]

There is now a conventional wisdom that the liberalization
of the capital account should be postponed until the
liberalization of the current account is complete. Whatever the

merits of this view in certain cases, that of Sri Lanka indicates that it is inappropriate as a general proposition. The danger noted by those concerned about the liberalization of the capital account is usually that of the *inflow*, which will reduce the profitability of industries producing tradeable goods and so undermine the chief benefit of trade liberalization: improved efficiency in the production of such goods, especially improved incentives for export. But the government of Sri Lanka had itself decided to seek a greater inflow in order to finance its investment programme. Given that decision, the consequence of continued controls on the capital account and domestic financial markets were twofold:

(a) By preventing capital outflows the appreciation of the real rate of exchange was larger than it need have been.

(b) And, by thwarting the creation of efficient markets for foreign exchange (especially forward markets), a policy of allowing the rate of exchange to float upwards was rendered infeasible. Such a policy, however, would have avoided the inflation attendant upon the capital inflows. The alternative policy of administratively adjusting the nominal exchange rate upwards is difficult to execute when changes in the economy are large.

Finally, in considering the failure to follow through on liberalization one cannot ignore the increased domestic unrest associated with civil disturbances of July 1983 and their aftermath. The government has become increasingly preoccupied with problems of civil order, problems of economic policy being put on the back burner.

LESSONS FROM THE SRI LANKAN EXPERIENCE

The experience in Sri Lanka shows that, contrary to what has been alleged from experience elsewhere (especially in Latin America), a democratically-elected government can undertake the liberalization of a highly distorted economy. Democracy is a system well suited to learning from experience, provided politicians are able to articulate the alternatives in a convincing way. This did, indeed, happen in Sri Lanka. Dismal economic performance led to the election of a government dedicated to removing its causes and the liberalization that it undertook was both substantial and, in certain respects, successful.

At the same time, the experience also underlines dangers.

First, a highly distorted economy that also suffers from a serious fiscal problem can be liberalized only with great difficulty. There is so much to do and every single distortion has lobbies in the private sector and in government, too, to defend it. It is all too easy for the government to find itself in a war of attrition, like the Battle of the Somme during the World War I, so losing its initial impetus. For this reason it is necesary to move to a competitive real rate of exchange, cut down the thicket of quantitative restrictions on imports and remove the fiscal imbalance decisively and quickly, so ensuring that improvements in subsequent economic performance will give increasing room for manoeuvre rather than finding it steadily reduced.[7]

Secondly, it is virtually impossible to liberalize successfully when the underlying fiscal problem is not resolved (or, still worse, as in the case of Sri Lanka, deteriorates further). In virtually all developing countries a large public-sector deficit entails either inflationary finance or foreign borrowing associated with a large current-account deficit (or both). Large domestic borrowing is generally infeasible. Under these conditions trade liberalization tends to be unsustainable.

As appears to have been the case in Chile as well, the liberalization itself worked well to improve trade and general economic performance. Where things went seriously wrong was in macro-economic policy, especially policy towards the exchange rate and capital inflows and, in the case of Sri Lanka, fiscal policy as well, the result being that the liberalization itself came under great pressure and was partially reversed. Since protection is usually introduced to deal with the balance of payments symptoms of a government living beyond its long-term means, liberalization cannot endure if the government continues to do so.

NOTES AND REFERENCES

1. T.G. Congdon, *Economic Liberalism in the Cone of Latin America*, Thames Essay No. 40 (London: Trade Policy Research Centre, 1985).

2. The author has discussed the influence of GATT agreements on developing countries and of individual developing countries on agreements in the GATT in 'Two-Edged Sword: Demands of Developing Countries and the Trading System', in Jagdish N. Bhagwati and John Gerard Ruggie (eds), *Power, Passions and Purpose: Prospects for North-South Negotiations* (Cambridge, Massachusetts: MIT Press, 1984), and Martin Wolf, 'Differential and More Favourable Treatment of Developing Countries and the International Trading System', mimeograph (1986). Paper prepared for the Conference on the Role and Interests of the Developing Countries in the Multilateral Trade Negotiations, sponsored by the World Bank and the Thailand Development Research Institute, Bangkok, 30 October to 1 November 1986.

3. Data on imports in 1984 are from *World Development Report 1986* (New York: Oxford University Press, for the World Bank, 1986) Annex Table 9 and *Financial Statistics: Taiwan District, the Republic of China,* February 1987, Taipei, Central Bank of China. Data on imports for 1970s are from *International Financial Statistics Yearbook 1986*, International Monetary Fund, Washington, and *World Tables 1976* (Baltimore and London: Johns Hopkins Press, for the World Bank, 1976).

4. On the role of outside institutions in liberalization, see Wolf, 'Timing and Sequencing of Trade Liberalization', *Asian Development Review*, Vol.4, No.2, 1986, pp. 1-24.

5. The issues are surveyed in W.M.Corden, 'Booming Sector and Dutch Disease Economics: Survey and Consolidation', *Oxford Economic Papers*, November 1984.

6. See Sebastian Edwards, *The Order of Liberalization of the External Sector in Developing Countries*, Essays in International Finance No. 156 (Princeton, New Jersey: Princeton University Press, 1984) and Lal, 'The Political Economy of Economic Liberalization', *World Bank Economic Review*, January 1987, pp. 273-300.

7. The need for speed in resolving the stabilization problem is emphasized in Wolf, 'Timing and Sequencing of Trade Liberalization', *loc. cit.*

Chapter 1

Socio-economic Inheritance
and Policy

THE SRI LANKAN economy at independence in 1948 was a relatively open economy which, compared with other South Asian and South-east Asian countries, had achieved remarkable standards of living both in terms of per capita income as well as in the quality of life as measured by certain indicators (Table 1.1). The economic structure has been described as being that of a classic dual export economy.[1] The modern plantation sector produced tea, rubber and coconuts; plantations were managed by foreign entrepreneurs and used immigrant labour. This sector co-existed with a traditional rural agriculture sector which employed the bulk of the working population. Rents from the 'modern' sector were siphoned off through export taxes and used to provide producer subsidies for the traditional paddy farmers and to fund high levels of social welfare expenditure, mainly consumer subsidies for rice and free health and educational benefits. These welfare expenditures accounted for a substantial proportion of gross domestic product (GDP) (Table 1.2).

In 1948 Sri Lanka's population was just over 6.5 million. It had large foreign-exchange reserves, a high level of general education and export crops of tea, rubber and coconut for which there was a thriving market. It was confidently expected that 'of all post-colonial nations, Sri Lanka would prove "the best bet in Asia"'.[2] Yet by 1977, when the United National Party (UNP) won a landslide election victory, most observers as well as the citizens of Sri Lanka had concluded that the country had failed to fulfil the promise of the 1950s. This is particularly true if Sri Lanka's performance is compared with other South-east Asian countries such as Malaysia and Thailand, let alone the star performers in the Gang of Four (Hong Kong, the Republic of Korea, Singapore and Taiwan). What went wrong?

To answer this question, two periods in Sri Lanka's history will be compared — 1883-1913 and from the Korean War

TABLE 1.1

Standard of Living in Some Asian Countries in 1960

	Per capita income ($)	Adjusted per capita income[a] ($)	Adult literacy rate (%)	Life expectancy at birth (Years)	Infant mortality (No. per 1,000 Births)
Sri Lanka	152	961	75	62	63
Thailand	95	446	68	51	na
Malaysia	280	888	53	57	na
Korea	153	631	71	54	62
India	73	428	28	43	na
Philippines	254	644	72	51	98

SOURCES: *World Development Report 1980* (New York: Oxford University Press, for the World Bank) and Robert Summers and Alan Heston, 'Improved International Comparisons of Real Product and its Composition: 1950-1980', *Review of Income and Wealth*, New Haven, June 1984, pp. 207-62.

[a]Adjusted to take account of differences in purchasing power. See Irving B. Kravis, *World Product and Income: International Comparisons of Real Gross National Product* (Baltimore: Johns Hopkins Press, 1982)

boom in the 1950s until the oil price shock in 1973. These periods have been chosen because they are times when world trade grew at a steady or even spectacular rate, thus providing an economic environment which was highly favourable for developing countries. Sri Lanka's response to these two major opportunities for reaping the gains from trade could not have been more different. The comparison will also highlight the importance of domestic policies (particularly those dealing with foreign trade, domestic prices and industrialization) in explaining Sri Lanka's poor economic performance from the mid-1950s onwards.

The growth of world trade in the last part of the nineteenth century and the early twentieth century (1883-1913) presented opportunities for the expansion of exports of tropical products which Sri Lanka exploited magnificently. During this period

TABLE 1.2

Government Expenditure in Sri Lanka as a Percentage of Gross Domestic Product, 1956-81

Category in	1951-52	1956-57[a]	1961-62[a]	1966-67[a]	1973	1977	1978	1980	1981
Social services	6.0	6.6	7.9	7.4	6.5	5.5	5.4	5.6	
of which:									
Education	–	3.6	4.8	4.4	4.0	3.3	2.8	3.0	
Health	–	2.4	2.4	2.3	2.0	1.7	1.7	2.2	
Economic services	8.0	4.7	5.8	5.2	3.9	3.4	3.8	5.1	
of which:									
Agriculture and irrigation	–	2.9	3.4	1.9	1.6	1.5	1.2	1.9	
Transfer payments	8.5	5.5	7.8	13.9	15.4	13.8	22.6	22.5	
of which:									
Food subsidies	5.5	1.0	3.6	5.6	4.6	3.6	5.4	0.5	
Total government expenditure	25.7	24.5	28.5	30.4	31.3	28.4	44.0	46.2	

SOURCES: Surjit Bhalla, 'Is Sri Lanka an Exception? A Comparative Study of Living Standards', in T.N. Srinivasan and Pranab Bardhan (èds), *Rural Poverty in South Asia* (New York: Columbia University Press, forthcoming); Karel Jansen, *State Policy and the Economy*, Research Report Series No. 12 (The Hague: Institute of Social Studies, 1982); *Annual Report*, Central Bank of Ceylon, Colombo, various issues.

[a]Fiscal years; other columns refer to calendar years.

trade grew at about 3.4 per cent per annum in current prices and about 3.8 per cent in volume.[3] Sri Lanka's export growth rate of 5.7 per cent per annum between 1883-1913[4] was the highest amongst the tropical countries which benefited from the growth of the world economy during this period. Its rate of per capita income growth must have been amongst the highest in the world and the quality of life of its population was by no means poor. Arthur Lewis estimated that in 1913, 'with one third of its children in school, Sri Lanka must have been at or near the top of the list for tropical countries'.[5] The fact that the economy depended on the growth of exports from the plantation sector and thus on the vagaries of volatile international markets did not, however, lead to great fragility in sustaining and raising income levels. To cope efficiently with the fluctuations in world demand for tropical exports, there must be flexibility in an economy so that the available factors of production can be transformed into the commodities in which the country has emerging comparative advantage. Sri Lanka's export sector demonstrated this flexibility in the nineteenth century, for instance, when the plantations switched to tea and coconuts after disease affected their coffee exports.

Helped by its integration into the world economy, the quality of life in Sri Lanka, as measured by some indicators, was well above other Asian countries in 1948. The life expectancy of its population was 54 years and was comparable then with a life expectancy in Japan of 57.5 years. Primary and secondary school enrolment as a percentage of the 5-19 years age group was, at 54 per cent, higher than in Korea (43 per cent). The infant mortality rate, at 77 deaths per thousand live births, was lower than in Malaysia (91 deaths per thousand live births). In 1960, Sri Lanka was still a relatively rich Asian country. Its per capita income at US$152 was twice what it was in India ($68), over 50 per cent greater than in Thailand ($97) and roughly equal to per capita income in the Republic of Korea ($154). If estimates of purchasing power parity, developed by the American economist Irving Kravis, are used to adjust per capita income, then in 1960 per capita income in Sri Lanka was higher than in either Brazil or Mexico.

By contrast, in the second great expansion of world trade that occurred in the three decades after World War II, Sri Lanka failed to take advantage of the opportunities presented by the rapid growth of international trade. Its relative export performance, compared with Malaysia and Thailand which have similar abundant natural resources and dual export economies, was particularly dismal in the 1970-82 period and was appalling compared with that of the Republic of Korea (Table 1.3). Sri Lanka's per capita income growth rate was only 2 per cent per annum between 1960 and 1978 and if Kravis-adjusted figures are used, it was negative at −1.1 per cent a year.[6] Its ratio of exports to GDP declined from 46 per cent in 1960 to 38 per cent in 1978. It has been noted that, 'other things being equal, this should have raised the Kravis-adjusted growth rate by increasing the weight of the non-traded to the traded goods in gross domestic product. Thus Sri Lanka's policies must have been more damaging to its economic growth than is generally recognised.'[7]

TABLE 1.3

Average Annual Growth Rate of Exports, Selected Asian Countries, 1960-70 and 1970-82

(per cent per annum)

	1960-70	1970-82
Sri Lanka	4.6	0.1
Malaysia	6.1	3.8
Thailand	5.2	9.1
Taiwan	23.7	9.3[a]
South Korea	34.7	20.2

SOURCES: *World Development Report 1980* and *World Development Report 1984* (New York: Oxford University Press, for the World Bank 1980 and 1984).
[a]Growth rate for 1970-78 period.

Nor, despite some assertions to the contrary,[8] has this poor growth performance been counter-balanced by significant gains in the quality of life. Surjit Bhalla, an economist at the World Bank, has shown that whilst the level of income and social welfare was better than the average for developing countries in 1960, Sri Lanka's performance in improving upon these levels (except for the death rate) is mediocre. He shows that, 'though absolute poverty was at a very low level in 1975, it had most likely increased since 1960'.[9]

By the mid-1970s, the relative failure of the Sri Lankan economy, arising from its attempts partially to withdraw from the world economy, was evident to the electorate if not to many outside admirers of the 'Sri Lankan model' of development. The new Government of Janius Jayawardena (United National Party) came to power in 1977; it was explicitly committed to reintegrating Sri Lanka into the world economy by liberalizing trade, prices and industrial controls and by attempting to replicate the development model that the Gang of Four had so successfully pioneered. The rest of this essay is concerned with assessing the nature, extent and consequences of this attempt to reintroduce an open export-oriented market economy in Sri Lanka and, in particular, to identify the reasons for its limited success. It will inevitably involve considerable discussion of the political economy of trade and industrial policies because the most likely explanation of Sri Lanka's relatively poor performance since about 1960 lies in its domestic policies rather than external circumstances or initial conditions.

As the policies of Sri Lankan governments altered with changes in the political parties in power, it would be useful to outline the broad sets of beliefs which determined each party's economic policies. Although the political motivations and origins of policies must be analyzed by political scientists, it is permissible to give the two major political parties a label as a convenient shorthand to discuss the major differences in their policies. The UNP is a 'rightist' party and the Sri Lanka Freedom Party (SLFP) and its coalition partners are the 'leftist' parties.

The swings in the political pendulum since Sri Lanka's independence can then be roughly categorized as follows:

    1947-56: UNP government (right).
    1956-65: Coalition led by the SLFP (left).
    1965-70: UNP government (right).

1970-77: SLFP government (left).

1977-87: UNP government (right).

Broadly speaking, in terms of trade regimes, the 'rightist' periods have corresponded with periods of movement towards liberalization of controls and the 'leftist' periods with a reversal of liberalization and the tightening of controls. The outcomes, in terms of economic growth, of these swings in the political pendulum since 1960 are summarized in Table 1.4.

TABLE 1.4

Rates of Growth of Gross National Product and Other Variables[a], Sri Lanka, Selected Years, 1960-83
(per cent per annum)

Item	1960-65	1965-70	1970-77	1977-82	1977-83
Agriculture, forestry and fishing	2.6	4.1	2.0	4.0	4.1
Mining and quarrying	1.0	13.9	27.3	7.6	7.6
Manufacturing	5.2	7.3	1.0	4.6	4.0
Construction	−1.1	17.6	−2.7	10.4	8.7
Services	4.8	4.3	3.7	7.2	13.0
Gross national product	3.3	4.4	2.8	5.8	5.6
Real national income	2.9	4.0	2.8	4.4	4.6
Population	2.5	2.3	1.6	1.7	1.6
Gross national product per capita	0.8	2.1	1.2	4.1	4.0
Real national income per capita	0.4	1.7	1.2	2.7	3.0

SOURCE: *Annual Report*, Central Bank of Ceylon, Colombo, various issues.

[a]Figures for gross national product, its components and national income are at 1959 constant prices in the first two columns and then at 1970 constant prices.

The periods when the 'leftist'-leaning SLFP was replaced by the UNP were periods in which GDP and per capita income accelerated. These changes in government were also accompanied by changes in the extent of *dirigisme*, with periods of UNP rule generally being those where some of the controls instituted by the SLFP were liberalized. Nor did the indicators of the quality of life necessarily worsen when there was a shift from the 'left' to the 'right'. Thus it has been estimated[10] that during the UNP's tenure of office in 1965-70 which was a period of rising per capita incomes, the absolute incomes of the poor also rose and income inequality was reduced. More recently, Surjit Bhalla[11] has put together comparable data on per capita real consumption expenditures between 1956 and 1984. These are shown in Figure 1 and graphically illustrate the adverse effects of the economic policies of the SLFP coalition between 1970 and 1977 as well as the correlation of rising per capita consumption levels with the relatively more liberal economic regimes associated with the UNP.

FIGURE 1.1

Real Consumption Per Capita, 1956-84

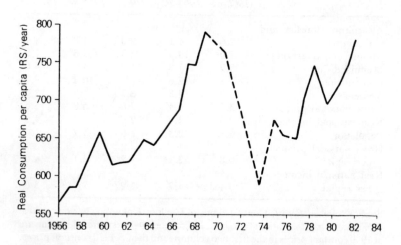

SOURCE: Surjit Bhalla, 'Is Sri Lanka an Exception? A Comparative Study of Living Standards', mimeograph, World Bank, Washington, July 1984, p. 36.

This essay is in five chapters. In this chapter the socio-economic inheritance in Sri Lanka and the policies which led to the economic liberalization have been analyzed, while in the second chapter the political economy of trade and industrial policies up to the liberalization of 1977 is examined. The political economy of the process of liberalization, the components of the liberalization package and their economic effects are considered in the third chapter. A number of analytical issues concerning the interaction of liberalization and stabilization, particularly in the light of the large capital inflows which accompanied the liberalization are covered in the fourth chapter. The timing and sequence of trade liberalization and its relationship to liberalization in other markets is also discussed in this chapter. In the fifth and final chapter the future prospects for Sri Lanka are considered.

NOTES AND REFERENCES

1. See Donald R. Snodgrass, *Ceylon: an Export Economy in Transition* (Homewood, Illinois: Richard D. Irvin, 1966).

2. Janice Jiggins, 'Dismantling Welfarism in Sri Lanka', *Overseas Development Institute Review*, London, No. 2, 1976. Quoting Sir Oliver Goonetilleke, Governor-General in 1955-62.

3. W.A. Lewis, *Growth and Fluctuations: 1870-1913* (London: Allen & Unwin, 1978).

4. *Ibid.*, p. 203.

5. *Ibid.*, p. 218.

6. Robert Summers and Alan Heston, 'Improved International Comparisons of Real Product and its Composition: 1950-1980', *Review of Income and Wealth*, June 1984, pp. 207-62.

7. Hla Myint, 'Distribution and Growth: What Have We Learned', mimeograph, World Bank, Washington, September 1984, p. 19.

8. See A.K. Sen, 'Public Action and the Quality of Life in Developing Countries', *Oxford Bulletin of Economics and Statistics*, Oxford, November 1981.

9. Surjit Bhalla, 'Is Sri Lanka an Exception? A Comparative Study of Living Standards', mimeograph, World Bank, Washington, July 1984, p. 36.

10. See Lal Jayawardena, 'Sri Lanka', in Hollis Chenery *et al*, *Redistribution with Growth* (Oxford: Oxford University Press, 1974); and Jiggins, *op. cit.*

11. Bhalla, 'Living Standards in Sri Lanka, 1970-1980: an Interpretation', mimeograph, World Bank, Washington, December 1984.

Chapter 2

Political Economy of Trade and Industrial Policy to 1977

THE EVENTS and forces leading to the 1977 trade liberalization must be understood in the context of two strands of Sri Lanka's political economy, one that goes back to the 1930s, when Britain ruled, and the other to the mid-1950s.

The first strand is Sri Lanka's commitment to large social expenditures. This commitment can be traced to the 1931 constitutional reforms of the Dhonoghmore Commission that yielded a measure of self-government. This led to political attempts to extend to the rest of the economy the level of welfare benefits already achieved within the plantation sector,[1] thereby placating the nascent electorate's demands for high levels of social welfare. Island-wide food subsidies, a legacy from World War II, became a major component of public expenditure for more than three decades, as did large expenditures on free education, which was introduced in 1944 along with free access to government-financed health services. By the late 1960s these burgeoning social expenditures were imposing a heavy burden on the public finances and by the mid-1970s they had led to an unsustainable fiscal position (Tables 2.1 and 2.2).

In the past, the traditional export sector had provided surpluses that could be taxed to finance these expenditures. Since the late 1950s, however, with the limited growth of Sri Lanka's exports (due in part to their high taxation),[2] the growing need to finance rising expenditure on social services and on expanding the public sector generally, there have been

Table 2.1

Government Finance 1954-84: Selected Data
(billion rupees)

	1954-5[a]	1958-9[a]	1964-5[a]	1967-8[a]	1970-1[a]	1977	1980	1982	1984
Revenue	1.2	1.3	1.8	2.2	2.8	6.0	14.1	17.8	37.7
Per cent of GNP[b]	21.6	22.5	24.2	21.8	23.8	16.0	21.1	17.9	24.9
Expenditure	1.0	1.7	2.2	2.9	3.9	8.3	30.3	37.9	53.6
Per cent of GNP[b]	18.9	29.6	30.0	29.0	32.9	23.0	45.6	38.0	35.4
Net cash deficit/surplus	0.1	-0.4	-0.4	-0.7	-1.1	-2.1	-14.8	-17.5	-13.6
Social welfare expenditure	0.4	0.6	1.0	1.3	1.5	na	na	na	na
of which:									
Education	0.2	0.3	0.4	0.4	0.5	0.9	1.4	2.0	2.6
Health	0.1	0.1	0.2	0.2	0.3	0.5	1.7	0.9	1.5
Food subsidies	0.4	0.1	0.4	0.6	0.6	1.4	0.3	0.1	0.1

Source: K.M. DeSilva (ed.), *Sri Lanka Survey* (London: Hurst, 1977) Table 3 Statistical Appendix for figures from 1954-55 to 1970-71. After 1970, figures are from Simon Rottenburg, 'Sri Lanka: the Public Finances', mimeograph, World Bank, Washington, September 1983, Tables 1, 7 and 9, *Annual Report*, Central Bank of Ceylon, Colombo, various issues and *Review of the Economy 1984*, Central Bank of Ceylon, Colombo.

[a]Fiscal year.

[b]Figures after 1970 are percentages of GDP.

continuing fiscal difficulties. Heavier export taxes were levied on the plantation sector to finance the growing paddy/rice and food subsidies, but the growing imbalance between the export taxes collected and the subsidies they financed can be seen in Table 2.3 (up to 1977).

TABLE 2.2

Public Deficit (net), Sri Lanka, Selected Years, 1960-84
(billion rupees)

	Public debt (net)	Internal debt	External debt
1960	1.9	1.7	0.2
1962	2.7	2.4	0.3
1964	3.4	3.1	0.4
1966	4.3	3.8	0.5
1968	5.7	4.7	1.0
1970	7.2	5.7	1.6
1972	9.5	7.1	2.4
1977	24.9	14.4	10.6
1978	30.9	16.4	14.6
1979	35.5	19.6	15.8
1980	51.7	29.4	22.3
1981	65.0	35.8	29.2
1982	80.2	45.6	34.6
1983	98.4	52.4	46.0
1984[a]	105.9	52.2	53.7

SOURCES: K.M. DeSilva (ed.), *Sri Lanka Survey* (London: Hurst, 1977) Table 3, Statistical Appendix for figures from 1960 to 1970. After 1970, figures are from Simon Rottenberg, 'Sri Lanka: the Public Finances', mimeograph, World Bank, Washington, September 1983, Table 11, *Annual Report*, Central Bank of Ceylon, Colombo, various issues and *Review of the Economy 1984*, Central Bank of Ceylon, Colombo.
[a]Provisional.

The second strand, which goes back to the 1950s, originates with the changing political ethos after a coalition led by the SLFP came into power in 1956. This was clearly a watershed in Sri Lanka's polity, as it marked a change in the political leadership from those who advocated almost *laissez-faire* policies to those who increasingly advocated *dirigisme.*[3] The UNP which was in power during 1948-56, was more closely associated with the Western-educated intelligentsia and was less prone to intervene in the classical export economy that

TABLE 2.3

Sri Lanka: Estimated Net Taxes and Levies from Plantation Crops Compared to Paddy/Rice Subsidies and Net Food Subsidies, 1960-1982
(million rupees)

	Tea	*Rubber*	*Coconut*	*Total net taxes on exports*	*Total paddy/rice producer and consumer subsidy*	*Net food subsidies and stamps*
1960	314	72	0	386	265	—
1961	336	42	0	378	263	—
1962	347	49	0	396	308	—
1963	365	43	0	408	304	—
1964	360	48	33	441	375	—
1965	342	49	102	493	331	—
1966	320	49	21	390	359	274[a]
1967	324	38	0	362	430	202
1968	338	22	132	492	560	296
1969	358	84	54	496	407	329
1970	348	98	53	499	526	327
1971	311	70	71	452	488	535
1972	335	22	75	432	408	526
1973	356	168	33	557	467	677
1974	210	363	112	685	799	951
1975	470	236	100	806	638	1,230
1976	395	283	3	681	508	938
1977	886	304	137	1,355	821	1,424
1978	3,590	1,076	545	5,743	na	2,163
1979	2,849	1,276	580	5,462	na	2,893
1980	2,135	1,219	394	4,428	na	2,022
1981	2,551	1,492	261	4,918	na	1,995
1982	1,777[b]	985[b]	108	3,357	na	1,739

SOURCE: Erik Thorbecke and Jan Svejnar, 'Effects of Macro-economic Policies on Agricultural Performance in Sri Lanka 1960-82', Development Centre mimeograph (Paris: OECD Secretariat, 1984).

[a]Amount is for entire 1960-66 period.

[b]Gross taxes rather than net taxes.

had evolved in Sri Lanka over a century. The SLFP coalition, led by S.W.R.D. Bandaranaike, owed its power to a part of the rural peasantry, the lower middle class and small urban industrialists, who were committed to an alteration of the export economy in two respects. First, they sought to diversify the economy and to end its 'foreign trade orientation' and, second, they wanted to ensure a measure of 'economic freedom' through the indigenization of the export-import trade and the expansion of what was then a small industrial base.[4] Thus it was after 1956 that a conscious effort was made to industrialize the country.[5]

Exchange controls were introduced in 1960 and 1961 in response to the deteriorating balance-of-payments situation in 1959. The first measures were introduced in August 1960. Exchange controls were applied to foreign travel, expenses for study abroad and capital transfers. This was followed by measures that applied to commodity trade.[6]

In 1960, the SLFP Government, led by Srimavo Bandaranaike following her husband's assasination, also adopted various measures of trade protection. These included high duties on imports of motor vehicles, petroleum products, textiles, tobacco, cigarettes and watches and high duties on exports of cinnamon, coir fibre and papain. Imports of consumer goods were most affected, declining by 25.2 per cent over the 1959 level, while imports of capital goods declined by 12.8 per cent and intermediate goods by 2.5 per cent. Overall protection levels were raised and the range of effective rates of protection was increased.[7] By 1962 all imports were subject to licences (quotas) except foodstuffs (largely a government monopoly), petroleum, fuel, fertilizer and pharmaceuticals.

The Bandaranaike Government's political platform committed it to industrialization and the foreign trade and exchange restrictions introduced in the early 1960s helped to realize this goal, if only fortuitously. These restrictions on trade raised the profitability of producing import substitutes. Industrial activity had been minimal in the past except for the production of a few items during World War II.[8] The boost to industrial activity in the early 1960s as a result of the exchange and import controls was subsequently supplemented by the introduction of explicit industrial policies. Industrialization behind protective walls became a part of the platform of the SLFP which, along with the Marxist parties, considered the existing structure of production to be a survival from colonial days. The 'economic independence', which it sought to complement political independence, was associated with industrialization. Moreover, economic arguments for industrialization behind protective barriers had become *au courant* at the time with the writings of Latin American structuralists. The prevailing pessimism among exporters, following the steady decline in the terms of trade from the very high levels reached during the Korean War boom, seemed to provide further arguments in favour of an 'inward-looking' development strategy.

Another important strand in the economic beliefs of the SLFP-led coalition was a commitment to the public ownership of major economic activities. This commitment, however, came to extend to most production activities, thus expanding the area of public ownership beyond the usual cases of infrastructure (with public goods aspects). For example, in the 1956-70 period, public corporations undertook an increasing number of industrial and commercial activities, including steel rolling, the production of hardware, cement, glass, fertilizers and milk. There was also public involvement in fisheries and in shipping. In addition, the state became active in foreign trade.[9] This commitment to public ownership also led to the nationalization of the plantations sector in 1975; this extended state control to the most important export activity in the country. The plantation sector had previously been considered among the best run in the Third World.[10]

By contrast, the UNP's attitude towards foreign trade had not changed since the 1950s. It emphasized a commitment to pursue the country's comparative advantage, including a commitment to support agricultural production and it favoured private enterprise over public ownership. It viewed tariffs primarily as a device to collect revenues, given the relative inelasticity of revenues from direct taxes. During its term in power from 1947 until 1956, the UNP neither attempted nor planned any change in the economic structure, for its power base was rural and agricultural. Each time the UNP has been in power, in 1947-56, in 1965-70 and from 1977, it has promoted agriculture through higher producer prices, the provision of infrastructure and reliance on the decentralized distribution of fertilizer and other farm inputs. By contrast, the SLFP during its tenure of office, neglected the agricultural sector. During the periods of SLFP rule, growth in agricultural output was low because of inadequate producer prices, reliance on price controls and the centralized distribution of farm inputs through multi-purpose cooperatives.

This bias against the agricultural sector was compounded by specific industrial incentives introduced by SLFP governments. For example, in 1961 the Development Division of the Ministry of Industries announced the following types of incentives:

   (a) the exemption of industrial profits from tax either partially or wholly;

   (b) the provision of development rebates to exempt from income taxes a percentage of the expenditures incurred in setting up an industry;

   (c) the introduction of depreciation allowances;

   (d) concessionary rates of duties on industrial equipment and raw materials;

   (e) government participation along with private capital in the establishment of small-scale private industry; and

   (f) protection of domestic industry through tariffs.[11]

The net effect was to raise the private profitability of industrial investments artificially, although with a bias against those with relatively lower rates of effective protection.

EVALUATION OF THE TRADE REGIME
   PRIOR TO 1977

After the introduction of trade restrictions between 1960-62, the trade regime became increasingly stringent as a number of well-known devices, including those listed in the following paragraphs, were adopted.

First, quantitative restrictions increasingly replaced tariffs as the major protective device.[12] The revenue tariff rates were raised and cash margins on letters of credit prescribed. Goods termed as 'luxury items' were most adversely affected. These included motor vehicles, petroleum products, certain categories of textiles, tobacco, cigarettes and watches. By the mid-1960s these tariff restrictions had been gradually converted into quantitative restrictions. By the mid-1970s, complete bans on 'luxury items' were common and the entire import bill was subject to quotas and licensing.

Second, a highly differentiated import tariff structure was introduced with tariff rates on imports ranging from 10 per cent to 300 per cent, differentiated according to the degree of competition with domestic substitutes. Between 1962 and 1965, the trade regime buttressed industrial policy. The protection provided to certain types of domestic industry increased as the tariff structure and quantitative restrictions became more discriminatory, with heavier protection on final goods by comparison with intermediate goods.

Third, the trade restrictions were accompanied by restrictions on foreign direct investment. Although the restrictions on remitting dividends and profits introduced through exchange control already inhibited foreign direct investment, further legislative controls were introduced in a White Paper issued in 1966. New criteria for permitting foreign direct investments were introduced; they included high domestic value added in the activity and the prospect of exporting the output of industries financed through foreign direct investment. A Foreign Investment Advisory Committee was set up in 1967 to approve and monitor foreign direct investment. By 1972 these provisions had become even more stringent, stipulating that such investment must not be used to replace existing technical skills and should provide enough foreign capital to offset the import content of projects. By this time, however, foreign direct investment had already been discouraged because of the number of nationalizations which had taken place; the nationalization programme had accelerated after the enactment of the Business Undertakings (Acquisition) Act of 1971.

To counteract the unfavourable effects of this Act, another White Paper was issued in 1972 to encourage private foreign investment. But these overtures were largely ignored by foreign investors. Meanwhile, the SLFP Government sought to register existing foreign investors as Sri Lankan companies to increase the degree of domestic control. A Companies (Special Provisions) Law was passed in 1974 which gave the government powers of nationalization over foreign-registered companies.[13]

Finally, there was a large increase in the government's direct control over trade and commerce, through nationalization and state entry into commercial undertakings. Monopoly rights to import essential goods, spare parts and building materials were granted to a number of public enterprises. They profited from the premia derivable from this monopoly power. As a consequence, the public sector expanded rapidly. The number of public enterprises increased from a handful in the early 1960s to more than 100 by the mid-1970s.

This galloping *dirigisme* had profound impacts on resource allocation, income distribution and growth. Clearly, the presence of high import duties, with little or no subsidization of exports, introduced enormous disparities in the incentive to undertake export promotion or import-substitution activities. An over-valued exchange rate was also maintained together with a stringent system of quantitative restrictions. The adverse effects on long-term growth and on its quality have already been noted.

With the return to power of a UNP government in 1965, a partial departure from the existing control regime was attempted in 1968. After the devaluation of sterling in 1967, the Sri Lankan rupee was devalued by 20 per cent. In 1968, the Foreign Exchange Entitlement Certificate Scheme (FEECS) was introduced; it was in effect a dual exchange-rate system.[14] The major effect of the scheme was to provide a favourable exchange rate for non-traditional exports and to impose additional rupee costs on imports, particularly of raw materials and capital goods. Under the FEECS, external transactions were divided into categories 'A' and 'B'. On the export side, exporters of category 'A' goods, which were the traditional exports of tea, rubber and coconuts received the official rate of exchange. On the import side, category 'A' included government imports of rice, flour, sugar, certain other essential consumer items like drugs, fertilizers, imports of government departments, cooperatives and other small scale producers. Category 'B' included non-traditional exports and all other 'non-essential' imports. Basically, category 'B' transactions were effected at an exchange rate lower than the official rate — initially, this was 44 per cent below the official rate. Foreign exchange earned by exports of category 'B' items were therefore entitled to a 44 per cent premium in rupees. Similarly, importers effecting transactions in category 'B' had to surrender a foreign exchange entitlement certificate; they were in effect, paying a premium rate for their imports.

The importance of the scheme was the liberalization that accompanied it. Many of the items classified as category 'B' imports (nearly 50 per cent of total imports) were liberalized and brought under open general licences. Although the FEECS was intended to function as an auction scheme in which the value of the premium was determined by supply and demand, this feature was abandoned after a month and the premium was fixed. The premium was raised to 55 per cent in 1969 and to 65 per cent in 1972 and remained at that level until November 1977. The import liberalization accompanying the scheme, however, was abandoned in May 1970, when the SLFP returned to power. All imports were once again subjected to individual licensing and the open general licensing system was abandoned.

The exchange-rate system in place at the time of the 1977 liberalization was thus characterized by a system of stringent exchange and import controls and a dual exchange rate in which the premium on items in category 'B' was set at 65 per cent.

With the progressive shift to quantitative restrictions on imports and stagnating exports, there was a further erosion of the government's traditional revenue base, whilst little headway was made in increasing the direct tax base. A number of attempts were made to increase direct tax revenues, beginning with an expenditure tax proposed by Nicholas Kaldor, the Cambridge economist. These attempts failed. As a consequence, the export sectors continued to be taxed to finance subsidies to consumers and to keep loss-making public enterprises afloat.

Although many observers noted the adverse effects on resource allocation associated with this sort of economic regime, it was not generally recognized that little, if any, improvement in income distribution and equity had been achieved in the 1960s and 1970s. If the economy had maintained a high rate of growth from the 1960s onwards, large improvements could also have been made in living standards and equity. As noted in Chapter 1, the initial conditions of Sri Lanka's per capita income and productivity, as well as its achievements in the social sphere, were already high compared with the rest of Asia. It could be argued that it was necessary to rely on public transfers to maintain acceptable levels of social welfare to offset the impact of interventions in the product markets that were creating large artificial rents for some producers. The interventions, however, had caused such a loss of efficiency that this redistribution was coming out of an overall 'economic pie' which was not growing fast enough to accommodate the 'entitlements' that had been created. The domestic system that had been established in the previous decade was on its last legs by the early 1970s.

NOTES AND REFERENCES

1. Since the early 1900s, plantation labour had been provided with housing, health care, limited educational facilities and some

measure of food subsidies. Nevertherless real remuneration to labour including these amenities was competitive by international standards and related to the productivity of the labour. In the non-plantation sectors, however, neither the same levels of productivity nor these social amenities were present.

2. Snodgrass, *op cit*. Donald Snodgrass argues that with an approaching land constraint, limits to the growth of tropical exports with existing technology were being reached by about the late 1950s.

3. A.J. Wilson in K.M. DeSilva (ed.), *Sri Lanka Survey* (London: Hurst, 1977) pp. 281-311.

4. This is not to assert that the UNP was not interested in transferring control of the import-export trade to the indigenous population. But they were much less committed philosophically than the SLFP to this aim. The UNP adopted the Imports and Exports Control Act of September 1954, which was aimed at safeguarding the government monopoly of some imports and the import-export trade for Ceylon nationals.

5. For example, the *Ten Year Plan* (1958-1968), proposed by the Mahajana Eksath Peramuna (People's United Front) had provided an investment programme for rapid industrialization. See H.N.S. Karunatilleke, *Economic Development in Sri Lanka* (New York: Praeger, 1971) pp. 77-80.

6. *Annual Report*, Central Bank of Ceylon, Colombo, various issues.

7. Effective protection rates try to measure the extent to which a domestic manufacturer can increase his processing costs as compared with a foreign competitor without exceeding the prices of imported products. They therefore concentrate on the relationship between the tariff and the value added rather than on the selling price. See Sydney J. Wells, *International Economics* (London: Allen & Unwin, 1969) p. 80. See also Karunatilleke, 'The Impact of Import and Exchange Controls and Bilateral Trade Agreements on Trade and Production in Ceylon', in Theodore Morgan and Nyle Spoelestra (eds), *Economic Interdependence in South Asia* (Madison: University of Wisconsin Press, 1969) pp. 285-304.

8. See Karunatilleke, *op. cit.*, p. 225. Government-owned factories were set up during the war to meet the needs of the domestic market as imports were limited because of the shortage of shipping. The output of these factories included plywood, quinine and drugs, leather and tanning, coir yarn, paper, ceramics, acetic acid, glass and steel. After the war, however, these wartime

22   *Impediments to Trade Liberalization in Sri Lanka*

industrial enterprises were closed down as they began to incur losses because of competition from imports. This enlightened policy was based on the advice of a government commission appointed in 1946 to evaluate the viability of government commercial undertakings.

9. A public corporation was even set up to produce and export cashew nuts.

10. D.M. Forrest, *A Hundred Years of Ceylon Tea, 1867-1967* (London: Chatto & Windus, 1968).

11. *Annual Report 1961*, Central Bank of Ceylon, Colombo, pp. 112-13.

12. The Central Bank's Annual Report for 1961 argued against the use of quantitative restrictions on the grounds that they introduced rigidities in resource allocation, led to arbitrariness in deciding between 'necessary' and 'luxury' goods and transferred income to quota holders. *Annual Report 1961*, Central Bank of Ceylon, Colombo, pp. 26 and 27.

13. *Sri Lanka: An Emerging Business Centre* (London: Economist Intelligence Unit, 1980) p. 53.

14. This was fashioned after the Pakistan Export Bonus Scheme, the auction features of which were initially adopted but later abandoned.

Chapter 3

Political Economy of the 1977 Liberalization

BY THE 1970s, the alignment of political and economic forces that had evolved from the 1930s to the 1950s had become clear. The SLFP-led coalition, which was in power for most of the 1956-65 period, had left its imprint on the economy.[1] The UNP which came into power during the 1965-70 period re-emphasized its support for the agricultural sector by raising producer prices; it provided large expenditures for agricultural development and attempted a partial liberalization of the trade regime in 1968 as described in the previous chapter. Despite that five-year interlude, however, the economy had undergone very significant changes, the effects of which excercised a dominant influence in the 1970-77 period. When the SLFP lost power in 1977, the economic structure was very different from what it had been before major trade controls were first introduced.

On the eve of the 1977 liberalization, the Sri Lankan economy was characterized by:

(a) a largely publicly-owned expanded industrial sector based on the production of import substitutes, and

(b) more quantitative restrictions on trade than in any previous period of Sri Lanka's economic history.

The plantation sector was in a depressed state, having been taxed in various ways to finance the burgeoning social expenditures and the promotion, since 1960, of loss-making public-sector-based industrialization. Moreover, in 1975 the plantation sector — the 'goose that laid the golden egg' —

was nationalized. The symptoms of an economy in crisis were further accentuated by increasingly poor growth performance, inadequate national savings and a pronounced tendency towards inflation which was assisted by budget deficits financed by the Central Bank.

Politically, too, the extension by decree of the life of parliament from five to seven years, the nationalization of the largest privately-owned newspapers and the perception that increased inroads into personal freedoms were being made, alienated public opinion. A sophisticated electorate had evolved over 40 years of universal suffrage and had traditionally refused to send incumbent governments back into power.

Janius Jayawardena, campaigning in the 1973-77 period, put forward a platform of economic liberalism that eschewed public ownership and state controls. Support for this position came from the traditional UNP elements, the Western-educated middle class élite and those who were dispossessed of lands (through the land reform) and urban property (through the housing property law), as well as from the vast majority of the populace who had begun to be disgruntled by the deteriorating economic situation aggravated, in 1973, by the oil price 'shock'. Nearly two decades of progressively stringent government controls had imposed high costs on the economy. Income growth averaged only 2.8 per cent a year in the 1960-77 period with only a few interludes of higher growth (during the 1965-70 period); 20 per cent of the labour force was unemployed by 1977; food shortages, a stagnant manufacturing sector and inflation rates in the 15-20 per cent range also characterized the economy.[2] Added to this, voters were afraid of losing democratic freedoms if the SLFP were re-elected.[3] Moreover, unlike the SLFP, the UNP did not have to depend on the support of private industrialists who had benefited from protection. There were also clear indications that foreign assistance would increase under a UNP government and that liberal economic policies would be supported by foreign aid donors. Finally, the SLFP Government was in disarray because of factionalism.

All these factors helped to bring about an overwhelming victory in 1977 for the UNP which was committed to liberalizing the economy. It would, however, be a mistake to think that the liberalization was solely the result of the change in government in July 1977, as some have claimed.[4] Discussions on the need for some liberalization in the economy as a matter of economic expediency were taking place as early as 1973. In that year, the UNP opposition adopted the liberalization of the economy as a part of its political platform. But, at the same time, the SLFP Government (Ministry of Finance) was also involved in tripartite discussions with the Central Bank and the International Monetary Fund (IMF). The SLFP Government in 1973 was, however, not ready to proceed with a substantial liberalization which would have included a devaluation, although they were willing to make some adjustments in tariffs and also to reduce some quantitative restrictions on imports. Their Marxist coalition partners, on the other hand, were violently opposed to any semblance of decontrol. Subsequently, it was the agenda of these Marxist parties which was adopted by the SLFP Government. The agenda included the nationalization of plantations, the redistribution of land and urban properties and the takeover of large enterprises including the dominant group of newspapers. These measures worsened the deteriorating economic situation and exacerbated a non-sustainable fiscal position and a decline in the terms of trade related to the 1973 oil shock. The measures did nothing to improve the imbalance between domestic income and the absorption of large capital inflows (see Chapter 4).

A number of factors helped to mobilize public support for the subsequent liberalization of controls undertaken by the UNP Government in 1977. First, the liberalization was perceived to benefit all groups, as compared with the concentration of the benefits, under the earlier regime, on those who could earn rents from the controls. Second, the newly-elected government's political mandate included a clear and strong commitment to reform. Third, there were immediate tangible benefits to consumers from liberalization measures — for example, the sweeping changes in quotas immediately increased the availability of consumer goods. Fourth, the removal of restrictions on foreign employment led to a steady flow of workers' remittances, while foreign capital inflows supported the liberalization measures by providing an adequate cushion of foreign reserves. Finally, trade union opposition was firmly handled. The rout of the union-supported political parties in the 1977 elections (especially the Marxist group) had sent a powerful message to the unions that the new government was fully in control of the political situation.

FEATURES OF THE LIBERALIZATION PACKAGE

An impressive list of measures was adopted by the UNP Government in November 1977. These included:

(a) The devaluation of the rupee by 46.2 per cent against the United States dollar and the unification of the exchange rate at the higher rate that applied under the extant dual rate. Subsequently a floating rate was adopted.

(b) Abolition of the system of pervasive exchange controls and quantitative restrictions and their replacement with tariffs.

(c) Removal of price controls except for a few 'essential' consumer goods. The procurement price of rice was raised by 21 per cent and the system of indiscriminate food subsidies was replaced by a food stamp programme aimed at the low-income segments of the population.

(d) Adoption of measures to attract foreign private investment, including changes in regulations governing the repatriation of profits and foreign investment licensing.

(e) The raising of domestic interest rates.

These reforms led to a number of basic changes in the trade regime and in the macro-economic situation.

First, the nominal devaluation reduced the bias against exports and other tradeable items that had been placed at a disadvantage under the dual exchange-rate system. Thus, for instance, the devaluation removed the 65 per cent nominal implicit tax on traditional exports that was implied by the dual exchange-rate system. This was counter-balanced to some extent, however, by the increase in duties on exports which accompanied the devaluation. The implicit subsidies to the 'A' category of imports were also reduced. In other words, with the devaluation, important aspects of the bias against tradeable items in general and exports in particular were reduced but not eliminated. As capital transactions were not liberalized, the aim of the devaluation was to affect the current rather than the capital account.

Second, in order to judge the effects on resource allocation, it is necessary to examine the extent of the effective devaluation implied by the tariff reforms that were introduced with the liberalization. The new tariffs were intended to replace the licensing system, which had been the main instrument used to restrict imports. The reforms led to the establishment of a six-band duty system that ranged from zero per cent for essential consumer goods (rice, flour, drugs) to a 500 per cent prohibitive rate on 'luxury' items. For the most part, the tariffs that were introduced were *ad valorem*. Although the new tariffs were higher, they eliminated the premia attached to quantitative restrictions thus reducing the nominal levels of protection; many of the earlier tariffs had been made redundant by the quantitative restrictions. While overall levels of effective protection were reduced, therefore, there was concern that the range of effective protection rates had increased under the new regime. This was perhaps an inevitable outcome of a rough and ready approach to tariff reform. A study of effective protection revealed that effective rates of protection were very high for many products.[5] Nominal tariffs on final products were consistently high with tariff inputs showing considerable variation.

Third, with the new export duties, the exchange rate for exports was not lowered as much as might have been implied by the devaluation. Thus, whilst the bias against traditional exports of the earlier dual exchange rate system was alleviated by the devaluation, their relative profitability *vis-à-vis* the production of import substitutes and other non-traditional exports did not rise as much as was implied by the reduction in the exchange rate. Furthermore, as a result of the threat of nationalization that had hung for a long time over the tree-crop sector, investment had been low and maintenance neglected since the mid-1960s. The small effective devaluation in favour of this sector had little effect, therefore, in increasing export earnings from traditional exports. The impact of the liberalization was not as beneficial as it could have been and Sri Lanka's share of the world market in the export of commodities such as tea, rubber and coconut products continued to decline steadily.

Fourth, a number of administered prices were decontrolled. Of these, the most significant price adjustment was for rice. Its producer price was raised by 21 per cent in 1977 and the price was converted from a ceiling to a floor price. Similarly, a number of other administered prices were raised. In addition, a number of food subsidies were removed. These included the reduction of the consumer subsidies on rice and the introduction of a food stamps programme in 1979 through which the number of subsidy recipients was sharply reduced and the total cost of subsidies was cut.[6] Public expenditure on food subsidies in 1977 had absorbed 23.6 per cent of government revenues and accounted for 4.6 per cent of GDP. By 1981, food subsidies absorbed 10.5 per cent of revenues, but represented only 0.5 per cent of GDP. Reduced subsidies were aimed only at the poorer half of the population; and for the rest of the population, food prices were raised to reflect the import costs of rice and flour. This reduction of consumer subsidies could potentially have had the effect of lowering government budget deficits significantly and hence the inflationary financing which had led to previous chronic macro-economic imbalances.

Fifth, measures were taken to promote private foreign investment. This began with the offer of inducements to participate in a newly created free-trade zone. Import-licensing requirements for foreign enterprises were relaxed and they were allowed free imports of capital.

Although these measures of economic liberalization marked a major improvement in resource allocation, they did leave an unfinished agenda. They needed to be supplemented in a number of ways if the original intent behind the liberalization was to be realized.[7] Additional measures should have included:

(a) a reduction in the variations between effective protective rates to help the movement towards a fully neutral trade regime;

(b) the establishment of an exchange rate which would continue both to keep exports competitive and to maintain an appropriate ratio between the prices of traded and non-traded goods so as to expand the tradeable goods sector;

(c) the liberalization of the domestic capital market and the removal of exchange controls;

(d) an increase in the flexibility in the labour market where rigidities had emerged because of the close links between the trade unions and the opposition political parties, such rigidities including minimum wages, restraints on dismissing workers and a complicated package of social security benefits; and

(e) removal of a number of continuing constraints on foreign direct investment.

AFTERMATH OF LIBERALIZATION

The aftermath of the liberalization measures can be analyzed in terms of the unfinished agenda. It will also be interesting to examine the policies adopted since 1977 to assess whether they have assisted the nascent process of trade liberalization or have undermined it. To do this, it is necessary to examine both domestic and international trade and payments policies.

By conventional standards the two years following the introduction of the liberalization measures were very successful (see Table 3.1). The economy rebounded to achieve rates of growth of gross domestic product of 8.2 per cent and 6.3 per

TABLE 3.1

Key Statistics for the Period 1977-84

(per cent per annum)

	1977	1978	1979	1980	1981	1982	1983	1984
Rates of Growth								
GDP (constant prices)[a]	2.9	8.2	6.3	5.8	5.8	5.0	5.0	5.1
Agriculture[a]	2.0	5.4	2.0	3.1	6.9	2.2	5.3	2.2
Mining and quarrying[a]	27.3	19.4	6.0	4.9	4.2	4.1	7.8	1.5
Construction[a]	1.0	7.8	4.6	0.8	5.2	8.0	1.0	-0.1
Services[a]	-2.6	28.3	20.9	11.0	-3.0	-2.0	6.8	5.8
Financial flows share in GDP								
(at current market prices)								
Net concessional aid	na	9.6	8.9	7.8	8.0	na	na	na
Net commercial borrowing	na	-1.4	0.2	5.7	4.9	na	na	na
Private remittances	na	0.8	1.4	3.4	4.5	na	na	na
Total aid and borrowing	5.5	9.0	10.5	16.9	17.4	na	na	na
Investment	14.2	20.0	25.8	33.8	27.8	30.3	29.6	26.3
Domestic savings	18.1	15.2	13.8	11.2	11.7	11.5	14.5	20.8
Foreign savings	-3.7	4.5	11.0	19.8	13.5	15.2	12.4	3.1
Public sector deficit	7.7	13.8	13.9	23.1	17.5	20.1	17.8	10.5
Current account deficit	3.5	4.5	11.0	19.8	13.5	11.8	9.1	0.5
Domestic government borrowing	2.9	4.7	6.7	13.9	7.4	9.9	7.4	2.0

Wages, prices and reserves								
Central bank cost of living index (% change)	1.2	12.1	10.8	26.1	18.0	10.8	14.0	16.6
Real wages (% change)	7.0	31.3	5.6	-9.6	-18.6	4.0	-3.6	
International prices (1977 = 100)								
Imports	100	113	136	171	173	162	151	
Exports	100	103	120	128	121	112	119	
Movements in foreign reserves (US$ million)	+183	+94	+48	-220	-33	-27	+1	

SOURCES: *Annual Report*, Central Bank of Ceylon, Colombo, various issues.

[a]The figures in the first column refer to the period 1970-77.

cent in 1978 and 1979 respectively and it continued to grow at 5.8 per cent in 1980; the annual average rate of growth for the period 1978-83 was 6 per cent. These growth rates contrasted with an average annual rate of growth of gross domestic product of 2.9 per cent in the 1970-77 period. This was perhaps to be expected in an economy where factors of production were less than fully utilized and which had, by and large, neglected its agricultural sector and created excess capacity in industry. The availability of considerable foreign-exchange resources from outside donors, the response of all sectors to improved incentives and the return of business confidence also infused a new dynamism in the economy.

The unemployment rate, which was estimated to be around 24 per cent in 1973, had declined to 15 per cent by 1980. In addition to an increase in domestic employment opportunities, the foreign demand for Sri Lankan labour — particularly semi-skilled workers — also rose. The removal of restrictions on employment abroad led to substantial increases in foreign employment, especially in the Middle East.[8]

Following the liberalization of trade, the new government launched a substantial public investment programme that was dominated by three 'lead' projects, largely financed by foreign aid. These were the accelerated Mahaweli programme,[9] a public housing programme and an urban development programme, which together led to a very substantial increase in public expenditure. In addition to their large claim on public resources, these programmes had long gestation periods and were competing for public funds with the traditional export sectors which were being rehabilitated. The Mahaweli programme, however, was largely financed by increased official capital aid flows. Although ultimately the judgment on the long-term viability of these projects must rest on their relative rates of return, compared with other investment alternatives in Sri Lanka, they nevertheless provided a boost to employment and the level of economic activity at that time. This was not, however, without considerable pressure on domestic prices, on the exchange rate and on the economy as a whole.

Mainly as a result of these projects, public investment which averaged less than 8 per cent of GDP in the 1970-77 period, rose to an average of 17 per cent in the 1980-83 period. Private investment also increased from 8 per cent of GDP in the 1970-77 period to 12 per cent in 1980-83. As a result of the increase in public investment, which was, however, unmatched by increases in public savings, budget deficits emerged. They were partly financed by foreign capital inflows, primarily related to the Mahaweli programme and partly by Central Bank borrowing. The budget deficit (taking account of grants) rose to 20 per cent of GDP by 1980 and was brought down to 10 per cent by 1983 only after considerable reductions in planned public investment.

Given the gap between public investment and saving together with insufficient production incentives and lags in the growth of exports as well as the continuing increase in imports, the balance-of-payments deficit on current account rose from 5.5 per cent of GDP in 1977 to 20 per cent in 1980. The deficit declined to 12 per cent of GDP in 1983 after some corrective measures had been undertaken.

The trade liberalization and the expansion of public investment programmes were undertaken at a time when the external environment for Sri Lanka's trade was unfavourable. The world recession reduced the demand for Sri Lanka's exports and worsened the terms of trade, whilst the accompanying rise in international interest rates raised the costs of commercial foreign borrowing. The combined adverse shock of these external events on the Sri Lankan economy has been estimated to be as much as 25 per cent of its GDP.[10]

By 1980, there were signs that the economic situation was worsening. The gains in competitiveness achieved through the devaluation were partially reversed and the new economic strategy that Sri Lanka had adopted with its bold liberalization measures seemed to be in jeopardy. Three factors are important in explaining these developments.

First, there was the worsening fiscal situation and a marked increase in the excess of domestic expenditure over income. The growth of consumption and investment exceeded the growth of aggregate output during 1979-83.[11] The major source of the 'imbalance' was the 'lead' projects which, together with the private investment that had been stimulated by liberalization, raised the total investment rate to 33.8 per cent of GDP at current market prices in 1980 compared with 14.2 per cent in 1977. Public current expenditure also increased despite the reduction in food subsidies which were largely offset by transfers to loss-making public enterprises. This substantial increase in public expenditure was largely financed by foreign borrowing. Domestic savings had remained fairly stable as increased private savings were offset by negative public savings (Table 3.2). The huge capital inflow also

TABLE 3.2

Domestic Savings and Capital Formation, 1960-83

	1960-65	1965-70	1970-77	1977-82	1983
Per cent of GDP:					
Domestic fixed capital formation	14.7	16.5	15.8	27.1	29.0
Domestic savings	13.1	13.1	13.4	13.0	14.5
Marginal propensity to save	13.3	13.6	12.8	8.6	28.2

SOURCES: J.J. Stern, 'Liberalization in Sri Lanka: a Preliminary Assessment', mimeograph, Harvard Institute for International Development, Cambridge, Massachusetts, July 1984, Table 2, derived from *Review of the Economy*, Central Bank of Ceylon, Colombo, various issues, and *Annual Report*, Central Bank of Ceylon, Colombo, 1983 and 1984.

financed a mounting current-account deficit on the balance of payments. As will be seen, this macro-economic imbalance had implications for the exchange rate and therefore for the gains from liberalization.

Second, there was the worsening external environment. The terms of trade fell from 102 in 1977 to 58 in 1980 (Table 3.3).

This, combined with the reduced volume of exports largely attributable to insufficient production incentives in the tree crop sector, contributed to a worsening of the trade balance. In the meantime, the absorption of the massive capital inflows through the accompanying real exchange rate[12] changes meant a further necessary deterioration in the trade balance. The appreciation of the real exchange rate is the mechanism which allows the absorption of foreign capital to take place.

TABLE 3.3

Sri Lanka's Terms of Trade[a], 1960-84

Year	Index (1978 = 100)	Year	Index (1978 = 100)
1960	185	1973	82
1961	170	1974	72
1962	178	1975	58
1963	161	1976	78
1964	133	1977	102
1965	142	1978	100
1966	137	1979	72
1967	120	1980	58
1968	117	1981	46
1969	110	1982	38
1970	106	1983	44
1971	98	1984	50
1972	94		

SOURCES: J.J. Stern, 'Liberalization in Sri Lanka: a Preliminary Assessment', mimeograph, Harvard Institute for International Development, Cambridge, Massachusetts, July 1984, Appendix, Table 2; *Recent Economic Developments*, International Monetary Fund Report No. SM/84/173, Washington, July 1984; *Annual Report 1984*, Central Bank of Ceylon, Colombo.

[a]Ratio of export prices to import prices.

Finally, in the face of both domestic- and foreign-induced macro-economic shocks (that is, the accelerated public investment and the world recession), revisionist thinking among some segments of the government led to a number of setbacks to the liberalization programme. Thus, rather than tackling the unfinished agenda from the 1977 liberalization, there was instead a rollback of what had been achieved.

In the first place, there was an appreciation of the real exchange rate as a consequence of the capital inflow that was linked to the large public investment projects in the early 1980s and also because of the appreciation of the United States dollar to which the Sri Lanka rupee was indirectly linked.[13] The appreciation in the real exchange rate as a result of the capital inflow was largely brought about by domestic inflation, which averaged 24 per cent per year during the 1978-83 period.[14]

Second, since the initial revision of tariffs in 1977, there had been a number of *ad hoc* changes in duties which, instead of reducing nominal rates of protection, had increased them. This had the effect of widening the range of effective rates of protection between different sectors. Duties on the traditional exports of tea, rubber and coconuts in 1983 were 25, 35 and 15 per cent respectively which, although lower than before 1977, were sufficiently high to act as powerful disincentives to production and exports. These rates were again revised in 1984, however, on the recommendations of the Presidential Tariff Commission. The fixed export tax on tea was reduced while the exemption rate for the *ad valorem* tax was raised. Similarly, the existing export duty on rubber was reduced. For coconuts the tax threshold was raised. On balance, the changes appear to have raised producer incentives.

A third factor was the increasing tendency to adopt non-price measures to promote exports, thus eschewing the commitment, which underlay the liberalization, to rely on the price mechanism. For example, the Export Development Board (EDB), which was established in May 1979, was empowered, *inter alia*, to regulate the sale and export of all products, to determine administratively the potentially successful exporters and to regulate insurance, freight and other related export marketing services.

Its activities are financed by taxes imposed on both imports and exports, but at a higher rate on the former.[15] The method of financing the export development fund by a 10 per cent tax on imports which carry duties above 50 per cent and by a smaller tax on a few non-traditional exports, is distortionary. Removal of these taxes, it could be argued, would promote export development more effectively by reducing import protection. The EDB, in combination with a number of financial institutions, also provides both equity and working capital to firms after scrutiny of their export potential. This makes export assistance arbitrary and some of the criteria adopted for providing assistance (such as the existence of high domestic value added) can damage efficiency. Moreover, this sort of measure further reinforces a distortion already inherent in the structure of Sri Lanka's export taxes which are, in many instances, graduated according to the degree of processing with a view to increasing domestic value added.[16]

In addition, the financial system has interacted with the trade regime to create differential incentives for exports and imports. These arise out of the activities of the EDB and a number of discount facilities offered by the Central Bank. Before the 1977 liberalization, Sri Lanka had a highly repressed financial system under a variety of controls, which included interest rate and credit ceilings, selective credit controls and differentiated access to Central Bank refinancing. The creation of money to finance budget deficits had also led to negative real interest rates. The public interventions led to a general stunting of the financial system which was characterized by insufficient depth and a narrow range of financial assets.[17]

With the trade liberalization, a number of measures to liberalize the financial system were also taken, two of which were significant in this respect. These were:

(a) the raising of regulated commercial bank interest rates to levels that led initially to positive real rates. (These rates, however, later became negative with the high inflation rates experienced in the 1979-83 period).

(b) permitting new foreign banks to set up branches to compete with existing local banks.

At the same time, however, the Central Bank continued with its previous methods of credit allocation to priority areas and it introduced new re-financing facilities for loans in favour of the agricultural sector, for manufacturing and for exports, but not for trade and tourism.[18] In addition, the government established the National Development Bank in 1979 to provide additional long-term resources. Thus, whilst interest rates were liberalized and a measure of competition fostered through the licensing of new commercial banks, the system of differential interest rates provided through various modes of re-finance was further extended and new sources of public funds were channelled to industry. Further, a new differential in the cost of credit was created in 1983 with the establishment of a re-discounting facility for export bills of small non-traditional exporters. Default risks on this facility are borne entirely by the Central Bank.

An overall evaluation of the liberalization of the financial regime presents a mixed picture. A measure of financial liberalization was counter-balanced by increased interventions in the form of increases in the differential costs of borrowings, differentiated ceilings (for example, limits on borrowing for consumption) and the attempt to allocate credit on the basis of a 'credit plan'.

As far as the labour market is concerned, its interaction with the trade regime had undergone two types of changes. After the liberalization of controls, workers' remittances became an important foreign-exchange earner second only to the earnings from tea exports. The other change was the erosion of trade union power as a result of the dismissal of government workers following a strike in 1980. Insofar as this helped to increase the flexibility of the labour market, it contributed to improved resource allocation. It should also be noted that as a result of the 1977 devaluation, the real wages of government employees declined by more than 30 per cent between 1979-81. The unions negotiated a wage indexation scheme which was at first on a monthly basis and later was extended to six months. In February 1984, there was a further whittling away of the indexation arrangements. The effect has been to contain wage increases in both the public and private sectors more than would otherwise have been possible. This has also helped to increase overall employment.

Policy initiatives on a number of fronts were inhibited by the civil disturbances of July 1983. The political consequences of this, as well as the continuing difficulties in solving the ethnic issue, have preoccupied the government. Protectionist forces both within and outside the government have received a new lease of life as a result of these difficulties and they have begun to claim that the liberalization was a failure.

Finally, there has been some concern about the impact of the trade liberalization and other associated policies on levels of economic welfare. After the introduction of the liberalization measures, there were reductions in food subsidies and in public expenditure on health and education. There has been considerable concern about the effects of these measures on living standards. Analysis of real consumption expenditures, however, shows that whilst living standards did decline in the immediate aftermath of the liberalization because of the full cost pricing of food and social services, they had recovered to their 1977 levels by 1980-81. Thus food consumption continued to show an upward trend after a dip in the 1977-80 period. Similarly, despite the reductions in subsidies to health and education, the demand for health and education services has continued to show an upward trend.[19]

Further confirmation of these favourable trends in living standards is provided by the increased production of rice and domestic output in general and the reduction in unemployment in particular. A full explanation of these developments must await further analysis. The preliminary evidence, however, does point to improvements in living standards as well as in the quantitative indices of growth in output and employment. This improvement can be attributed to better resource allocation and increased investment in an economy which, because of 'policy induced' distortions, had previously been operating well below its full operating capacity.

It would seem, therefore, that while the initial impact of the liberalization measures was to increase efficiency, there has since been a significant rollback of the gains made because of the imbalances in the domestic economy as well as developments in the international environment. The continuation of trade-policy reforms as well as improvements in exchange-rate and fiscal management have been limited and little effort has been made to maintain the gains, let alone attempt to complete the unfinished agenda arising out of the 1977 liberalization. To some extent political factors have inhibited new policy initiatives. But, despite the concern that living standards have declined following the liberalization, there is some evidence that they have improved.

NOTES AND REFERENCES

1. The UNP held power briefly, in 1960, under Dudley Senanayake as Prime Minister.

2. The Colombo consumer price index considerably under-stated the actual level of inflation. It showed inflation rates no higher than 10 per cent. The index was based on a survey of workmen's expenditure of 1947. It had many subsidized items in it and the Department of Statistics kept 'adjusting' the weights. The fact that wage contracts were geared to the index made it a politically sensitive variable.

3. The defeat of Mrs Ghandi in the 1976 Indian elections, ascribed to her attempt to curtail democratic freedom, was thought to have set an example worthy of emulation by Sri Lankan voters.

4. Joan M. Nelson, 'The Political Economy of Stabilization in Small, Low-income and Trade-dependent Nations', mimeograph, Overseas Development Council, Washington, July 1984.

5. A.G. Cuthbertson and Mohammed Z. Khan, 'Effective Protection to Manufacturing Industry in Sri Lanka', mimeograph, Ministry of Finance and Planning, Colombo, 1981.

6. Recent evidence indicates that *per capita* real consumption of food which had declined to the lowest level in 1974 began to recover up to 1976, fell again following the liberalization and has recovered since then. See Bhalla, 'Living Standards in Sri Lanka, 1970-80: an Interpretation', *loc. cit.*

7. President Jayawardena's plan was to make a Singapore out of Sri Lanka. Ironically, Singapore's Prime Minister, Lee Kuan Yew, had campaigned in the 1972 election claiming that he had to be elected to ensure that Singapore was not to go the way of Sri Lanka at that time.

8. *Socio-economic Survey 1973* and *Socio-economic Survey 1980* (Colombo: Central Bank of Ceylon, 1974 and 1981).

9. A river basin development scheme to provide irrigation and power. It is referred to as an 'accelerated' programme as the original scheme, planned to take 30 years to complete, was reduced to about eight years.

10. Bela Balassa and Desmond McCarthy have estimated that the combined external shocks on Sri Lanka arising out of adverse terms of trade, high interest rates and reduced demand for exports was 25 per cent of GDP in the 1979-81 period, as compared with an average of 5 per cent for developing countries as a whole. See 'Adjustment Policies in Developing Countries', mimeograph, World Bank, Washington, July 1984.

11. Consumption in real terms grew at an average annual rate of 7.5 per cent during 1978-83 while investment grew by 9.7 per cent over the same period.

12. Defined as the relative price of tradeable goods as a whole to that of non-tradeable goods as a whole. Tradeable goods are exports together with import substitutes.

13. Although the external value of the rupee is kept as a managed float, the trade weight of United States dollar-denominated transactions appear to dominate the basket.

14. Central Bank price index. See Deepak Lal, 'The Real Exchange Rate, Capital Inflows and Inflation: Sri Lanka 1970-1982', *Weltwirschaftliches Archiv*, Kiel, December 1985, for an analysis of the link between capital inflow, the real exchange rate and inflation in Sri Lanka.

15. This, of course, increases the bias against exports by raising the protection offered to import substitution.

16. Cuthbertson and Khan, *op. cit.*

17. Deena Khatkate, 'Anatomy of Financial Retardation in a Less-developed Country: the Case of Sri Lanka, 1951-76', *World Development*, Vol. 10, No. 9, pp. 829-40.

18. Special measures were being adopted to support trade and tourism through the Export Development Board.

19. Bhalla, 'Living Standards in Sri Lanka, 1970-80: an Interpretation', *loc. cit.*

Chapter 4

Analytical Issues of the Liberalization

THE 1977 PROGRAMME of trade liberalization in Sri Lanka and its subsequent partial reversal give rise to a number of interesting analytical issues. The first concerns the relationship between trade liberalization and macro-economic stabilization. The second raises the role of exchange-rate movements during a trade liberalization, in particular when the liberalization is accompanied by large inflows of foreign capital. The third concerns the speed of trade liberalization and the related question of the proper sequencing of the liberalization of other controlled markets in the economy and, in particular, the capital market. These issues are discussed in turn, followed in the final chapter by an assessment of the prospects for future Sri Lankan efforts at liberalization.

TRADE LIBERALIZATION AND ECONOMIC STABILIZATION

It is ironic that the trade liberalization of 1977 which was introduced partly because of macro-economic difficulties should have been partially undone by the creation of new and yet more serious imbalances in the overall economy. The 'old' macro-economic imbalances were reflected in a chronic imbalance between total domestic investment and savings or, equivalently, between total domestic expenditure and income. This was reflected in both a serious fiscal crisis and a chronic balance-of-payments problem which was suppressed through tight exchange and import controls. The various reductions in consumer and producer subsidies in 1977 were meant to reduce domestic expenditure as well as to improve the fiscal balance. The trade reforms and accompanying devaluation were designed to improve the growth rate in the economy and thence future levels of income through which the existing standards of welfare payments could be financed. Both measures were also meant to improve the incentives to producers of export goods. In addition, domestic expenditure was switched away from tradeable goods in an effort to improve the balance of payments.

The trade liberalization, even though incomplete, did have the effect of rapidly improving the economy's growth performance and it should have helped to cure the chronic imbalance between domestic expenditure and output. The improvements in the fiscal balance arising from the cutback in subsidies were, however, counter-balanced by the massive increases in public expenditure to finance the 'lead projects' and to cover the losses of public enterprises. Though a considerable part of the resulting fiscal deficit was financed by capital inflows, these inflows created many new problems of economic management and, paradoxically, worsened the economy's macro-economic balance (as it will be argued in the next chapter). Thus, whilst the economy was being partly liberalized, it was not being stabilized.[1]

This macro-economic imbalance was aggravated by the movements in the exchange rate. The capital inflows and the link to the United States dollar led to an appreciation of the rupee, which reduced the export competitiveness gained from the devaluation. Thus, the real exchange rate appreciated by 20 per cent between 1978 and 1982. Moreover, with the expansion of construction activity on the 'lead' projects, non-traded goods prices increased rapidly as a further offset to the devaluation. Thus, the switching of domestic expenditure from traded to non-traded goods was thwarted by the real exchange-rate appreciation that arose from the capital inflows.

In addition, the reform of the financial markets, which must play a prominent part in any effective stabilization programme, was neglected as the government attempted to ease the financing of the public-sector deficit by imposing ceilings on interest rates. In fact, government controls on private financial markets combined with the large public-sector borrowing programme to crowd out private investment.

LIBERALIZATION AND CAPITAL INFLOWS

Although the financial markets continued to be regulated after the trade liberalization, Sri Lanka's creditworthiness increased as more viable economic policies were adopted in 1977. Commercial borrowings from abroad increased and there was a large inflow of aid. In addition, there were substantial private remittances from Sri Lankans working abroad.

The effect of this massive capital inflow, which expanded from about 5 per cent of GDP in the early 1970s to over 17 per cent in 1981, was equivalent to a 'Dutch disease' type shock to the Sri Lankan economy. The difficulties in economic management that many countries have experienced in absorbing large foreign-exchange windfalls, whether in the form of natural resources, rents, resources from primary product price booms or large inflows of foreign capital, have been copiously analyzed.[2] The essential point to be emphasized is that if these foreign-currency inflows are to be absorbed by the domestic economy, then there must be an appreciation of the real exchange rate which, in turn, allows a trade deficit equal in size to the inflows to materialize. For a given size of capital inflow the accompanying trade deficit and real exchange rate appreciation are an equilibrium phenomenon. As long as the inflows continue, attempts to reduce the trade deficit through a devaluation will only lead to a further rise in the price of non-traded goods to restore the previous equilibrium real exchange rate.

Thus the only relevant question, if the capital inflow is to be absorbed, is whether the required appreciation of the real exchange rate is brought about by a fall in the domestic prices of traded goods or a rise in those of non-traded goods. In Sri Lanka it was the latter inflationary channel through which the real exchange-rate appreciation occurred. But if, instead, the nominal exchange rate had been raised or, better still, the level of taxes on traded goods had been reduced, the required appreciation of the real exchange rate could have occurred without any rise in the general price level. As a consequence, the adverse expectations about the sustainability of the trade liberalization which actually accompanied the capital inflows, could then have been avoided.

This assumes, of course, both that the capital inflows could be sustained and that they were desirable in the sense that they could be used on activities with positive rates of return. Conclusions regarding the appropriate real exchange rate and the overall development strategy turn on these two issues.

The sustainability of the commercial capital inflows will depend, in part, upon the future prospects for the Sri Lankan economy. If lenders perceive that a borrowing country is productive enough at least to yield sufficient returns to cover the repayment and interest costs and also that the country's future export growth prospects are bright enough to allow it to service its debt in foreign exchange, then there can be little doubt that the commercial inflows will be sustainable. As regards the official aid inflows, their sustainability depends upon political factors in donor countries, as well as on the social returns from the public investment programmes which they help to finance. In practice these returns have not been high.[3] Moreover, in determining the desirability of these inflows, even if their level is sustainable, it is important to consider their indirect costs to the economy as a whole. The rise in the real exchange rate which necessarily accompanies both the public and private capital inflows makes it difficult to develop new exports. It also implies that export growth will be lower than it would otherwise have been and lower than that required for the growth path of the new open economy brought about by the trade liberalization, once the capital inflows cease. Moreover, as the public investment programme financed by the inflows made intensive use of non-traded goods, the required real exchange-rate appreciation during the period of inflows was higher than if an investment programme which was more 'neutral' with respect to the use of traded and non-traded goods had been undertaken.

Much of the inflation, appreciation of the real exchange rate and increased current account and budget deficits required to effect the large foreign transfer of resources which have characterized the Sri Lankan economy since the 1977 trade liberalization, can thus be seen to result from the large capital inflows, mainly into the public sector. These inflows have worsened the problems of achieving long-run macro-economic stability in the economy. Whilst any increment of resources (net of repayment and interest costs) must necessarily improve economic welfare, the optimal policy response to such large inflows, particulary when they are tied to low return public investments, is hard to bring about. It could well have been better, therefore, for Sri Lanka to have completed the trade and financial liberalization before undertaking such large foreign-financed public-sector investments.

TIMING AND SEQUENCING OF THE
    LIBERALIZATION

The major point to make about the timing of the trade liberalization was that it was out of phase with conditions in the world economy. Thus, if a liberalization effort had been undertaken in, say, 1973 and sustained up to the 1980s, it would have ensured a higher and more permanent employment growth path. On the other hand, the rapid effect of the 1977 liberalization in raising the growth rate of the economy shows that, even in an unfavourable external environment, there are enormous efficiency gains to be reaped by reducing trade distortions.

Moreover, the rapid initial liberalization of quantitative restrictions was not followed up by an equally rapid reduction of tariffs. This incomplete liberalization was soon overtaken by the macro-economic crisis and a policy paralysis ensued, except for short-term actions to meet the crisis. Thus, in the 1982-83 period, drastic cuts were introduced in the public investment programme.

The first two steps in the planned sequencing of the trade liberalization, from the devaluation to the removal of quantitative restrictions, worked well. The next step required to achieve neutrality in the trade regime through tariff reductions was, however, postponed. It is clear, in retrospect, that this gradualism reduced the chances of completing the reforms. It is true that, with the establishment of the Tariff Review Committee in 1977 and its transformation into the President's Tariff Commission in 1980, some attempts were subsequently made to ward off pressures for protection. Thus, tariff-reform measures undertaken in the context of the 1985 budget, were intended to reduce the range of effective rates of protection by establishing a narrower band tariff structure. These reforms, however, were deficient in two respects. First, some 35 items produced by public enterprises continued to enjoy high rates of protection. Second, reduced tariffs on such items as imported machinery for producers of exports biased production in favour of higher capital intensity. The need to provide these special provisions for particular interest groups raises the question of whether it would not have been better to have opted, at the beginning, for a more complete liberalization.

LIBERALIZATION IN OTHER MARKETS

There was no serious effort to liberalize the domestic capital market or to open up the capital account of the balance of payments. This would not, of course, have been easy, given the exchange-rate uncertainty that prevailed in the period. Also, the order of liberalization adopted in which the current account was liberalized first, seems to be the appropriate pattern if the experience of liberalization in other countries is to serve as a guide.[4] Whereas in other countries, however, the liberalization of the capital account as well as the current account has sometimes led to capital inflows which brought about an appreciation of the real exchange rate, a similar result occurred in Sri Lanka without the liberalization of the capital account because of the official capital flows linked to the 'lead' projects. Such an appreciation works against the economy's long-run need to increase the production of traded goods.

An opening-up of the capital account would have allowed at least some of the foreign-currency inflows to be translated into foreign assets which would have dampened the real exchange-rate appreciation. Appreciation of the real exchange rate, however, is the mechanism by which increases in foreign-exchange resources are absorbed into the domestic economy. The difficult issue for economic management is the extent, and even the direction, in which the exchange rate should be altered in a managed exchange-rate system during a trade liberalization process which is accompanied by large inflows of public or private capital. Because of this uncertainty, a case can be made for adopting a freely floating exchange rate with a concurrent liberalization of both the current and the capital accounts of the balance of payments.[5] The efficient working of a floating rate, however, requires the creation of a forward market for foreign exchange which, in turn, would entail the freeing of controls on the domestic financial market.

The domestic financial market was, it is true, partially liberalized insofar as interest rates on commercial bank loans and deposits were permitted to be determined in the market. At the same time, however, the Central Bank increased its interventions in the financial markets through the establishment of credit ceilings and a variety of discount facilities differentiated by product and specific economic activities.

A proper reform of the financial system to complement the trade liberalization thus remains an important aspect of the unfinished agenda. The measures of reform which are needed would include the following:

(a) positive real interest rates should be established and maintained, both to raise the level of private savings and to facilitate their mobilization by the financial system.

(b) the costs of government borrowing should be increased to equal the opportunity cost of its funding. In this respect, the attempt to float domestic bonds was a welcome change in policy, despite the restrictive requirement that these bonds must not be held by other public financial institutions.

(c) there should be substantial reduction in the number of refinancing facilities and the costs of credit for different rediscount facilities should be equalized.

(d) aggregate demand should be stabilized by reducing the fiscal deficit rather than by relying on overall credit ceilings.

Taken together, these measures would allow efficient financial intermediation between all savers and borrowers in the economy rather than just between the government and the public.

Finally, there is the effect of the liberalization on the labour market which was partially liberalized by allowing Sri Lankan workers to seek employment abroad. Although, in general, real wages first increased and then declined as a result of the overall movements in the economy previously described, the relative liberalization of the labour market led to a change in relative wage rates. The increase in foreign demand for semi-skilled labour caused the domestic wages of such labour to rise relative to other categories of labour. It is difficult to trace the interactions between the labour market and the trade regime except to say that the liberalization increased the overall demand for labour. A considerable part of the employment created, however, was caused by the large public investment programme which supported only transitory employment arising out of the temporary construction boom.

NOTES AND REFERENCES

1. Anne Krueger has argued that 'more efforts to liberalize trade sectors of developing countries have floundered upon the failure of accompanying anti-inflationary programmes than any other single factor'. See Anne O. Krueger, 'Problems of Liberalization', in Arnold C. Harberger (ed.), *World Economic Growth* (San Francisco: Institute for Contemporary Studies, 1984).

2. See W.M. Corden, 'Booming Sector and Dutch Disease

Economics: Survey and Consolidation', *Oxford Economic Papers*, November 1984 for an analytical survey of this literature.

3. See J.J. Stern, 'Liberalization in Sri Lanka: a Preliminary Assessment', mimeograph, Harvard Institute for International Development, Cambridge, Massachusetts, July 1984.

4. Sebastian Edwards, 'The Order of Liberalization of the External Sector in Developing Countries', mimeograph, National Bureau of Economic Research, New York, June 1984. For another view which argues for liberalizing both capital and current accounts simultaneously, as well as adopting a floating exchange rate, see Lal, *The Real Effects of Stabilization and Structural Adjustment Policies: an Extension of the Australian Adjustment Model*, Staff Working Papers No. 636 (Washington: World Bank, March 1984).

5. See Lal, *ibid.*

Chapter 5

Future Outlook for the Sri Lankan Economy

THE FORECAST for the Sri Lankan economy depends upon a number of factors. They can be grouped into two broad categories, namely:

(a) the allocation of resources which will determine whether Sri Lanka can continue on its new higher post-1977 growth path and

(b) factors relating to economic stabilization.

Obviously, the two sets of issues are inter-related as the real exchange-rate implications of stabilization affect the long-run allocation of resources to the efficient production of tradeable goods. But it is inconceivable that a respectable rate of long-term growth can be maintained without taking steps to correct the macro-economic imbalance arising from the fiscal deficit which has been pronounced since 1980. To be sure, a number of stabilization measures were undertaken in the 1982-85 period and fortuitous circumstances, such as increased export revenues from tea,[1] have helped to postpone the adjustment. In addition, there has been progress in trade liberalization with some tariff reforms introduced in 1985 which narrowed the range of nominal tariffs and reduced export duties. On the other hand, more adjustment is needed; the sooner the better.

The unfinished agenda of the 1977 liberalization discussed in earlier chapters contains most of the measures required to achieve sustained higher rates of economic growth.

First, the trade reform needs to be completed. This requires a further reduction in categories of import tariffs and hence in the range of effective protection rates. After the 1982-85 reforms, the range of nominal rates of protection narrowed to a 5-75 per cent band. Further reductions in duties on traditional exports may be needed, however, in order to move towards neutrality in the trade regime between imports and exports. In this regard, continued adjustment of the exchange rate is vital. In addition, the exceptions granted to some 35 products against the lowering of tariffs and the reduced duties on some imported machinery (see Chapter 4), violates the need to move towards neutrality. The raising of the Business Turnover Tax on imports also offsets the tariff reduction and maintains protection. These deficiencies in the 1985 reforms amount to a bias against exports. This bias needs to be removed to improve overall resource allocation, resuscitate the traditional export sector and resume a path of export-led growth which has been the mainstay of Sri Lanka for over a century since its entry into the world economy. This would imply that more tariff changes are needed than those introduced in the 1985 budget.

Second, export promotion policies need to shift from reliance on non-price measures, such as concessionary loans and the licensing of exports on the basis of a domestic value added criterion. Moreover, to promote exports by levying import taxes is self-defeating, as the resulting rise in protection for imports is an implicit tax on exports. In general, export dynamism will not be restored by the actions of agencies such as the Export Development Board, but only through changes in the overall trade regime and the adoption of an appropriate exchange rate. In this context, it is also important to reiterate that the level of export taxation on traditional exports, such as tea, continues to be excessive despite the 1985 reforms. Export taxes have partly been designed to siphon off high export revenues. But such taxes distort incentives and inhibit the growth in production of those products in which Sri Lanka continues to have a comparative advantage.

Third, administered prices need to be freed, particularly for public-sector output. Thus, the government should seriously consider the choice of either freeing the output prices of public corporations and privatizing them or of dismantling these enterprises altogether (as was done so courageously after World War II). Clearly, the large and unprofitable public sector has not only caused serious damage to resource allocation but has also absorbed the savings that have been made through the reduction of consumer subsidies. It is difficult to conceive how a dynamic and viable economy can be developed as long as the waste of resources associated with public-sector corporations, which has become such an endemic feature of the Sri Lankan economy, is allowed to continue.

As regards the measures needed to stabilize the economy, it will be necessary, first, to reduce further the growth in public expenditure. There has been a significant cut in expenditure on the 'lead' projects — the Mahaweli programme and the urban development and public housing programmes. But more cuts in public-sector spending are needed to restore a balance between nominal demand and real income growth. The budget deficit still accounts for 10 per cent of GDP. Appropriate reductions in public expenditure would also have the further effect of reducing the balance-of-payments deficit to a level which can be sustained by the reduced level of external assistance that can be expected with the completion of the 'lead' projects.

The current-account deficit also reflects an excess of investment over savings which has been financed by foreign savings, primarily linked to the 'lead' projects. The slowing down of public investment expenditures in the mid-1980s contributed to the reduction in the current account deficit, as did the increase in the rate of domestic savings from 11.2 per cent of GDP[2] in 1980 to 20 per cent in 1984, although it is not clear whether the increase in savings is permanent. If foreign capital inflows decline in the future, as seems likely, the current rate of domestic savings will have to be increased further on a permanent basis to sustain future rates of growth comparable to those of the 1977-82 period. Even if there is a reduction in the economy's incremental capital output ratio with the completion of the 'lead' projects, it is unlikely to be sufficiently large to permit domestic savings alone to finance the new lower level of aggregate investment required to maintain the 1977-82 growth rate. The forecast for the future is thus crucially dependent on the economy's ability to raise the domestic savings rate. That ability is now constrained by two factors, namely the subtraction from private-sector savings of the public dis-savings represented by large public-sector deficits[3] and the inadequate incentives for domestic savings.

Finally, partly because of the rise in domestic prices resulting from an excess demand for non-tradeables and also because of increases in nominal wages in new contracts,[4] the domestic cost structure has been raised, thus vitiating the gains from the 1977 devaluation. The 'lead' projects, by putting enormous pressure on non-traded goods prices, have raised the real exchange rate, reducing the competitiveness of exports.[5] To the extent that official capital flows have helped to finance the balance-of-payments deficit, exchange-rate adjustments can be postponed, but there is no guarantee that they can be avoided for very long. Certainly, the successive nominal depreciations of the rupee since the adoption of a more flexible exchange-rate system have not been adequate to offset domestic inflation. Thus, further adjustments of the nominal exchange rate to realign the domestic cost structure and maintain the competitiveness of exports must also be a basic goal of policy.

From the above analysis, it must be clear that, if the current policy framework is not changed, the outlook for the Sri Lankan economy is not very bright. The 1977 liberalization which was achieved with considerable commitment, skill and political will, is in danger of being completely reversed; this would be unfortunate, indeed, for the future of the economy. But if that does happen, the conclusion to be drawn from Sri Lanka's bold experiment should not be that the economic liberalization itself failed, but rather that the authorities failed to stabilize the economy and that it was this that led to the reversal of the liberalization.

NOTES AND REFERENCES

1. With India banning tea exports until May 1984, Sri Lanka was able to command higher prices.

2. At current market prices.

3. The public-sector deficit amounted to 10.2 per cent of GDP (at current market prices) in 1984.

4. An example is the April 1984 contract that raised the wages of state plantation workers by 40 per cent.

5. As noted in Chapter 4, the rise in the real exchange rate has come about in Sri Lanka through a rise in the price of non-traded goods, rather than through a fall in the domestic price of traded goods. The increases in construction-sector prices associated with the 'lead' projects have put additional pressure on the prices of non-traded goods over and above a 'neutral' increase in aggregate demand. Thus, while the GDP deflator increased by 226 per cent between 1977 and 1982, the construction-sector price index increased by 523 per cent over the same period.

List of References

THIS list contains only the more important references cited in the text. The reader should refer to the Notes and References at the end of each chapter for more complete bibliographical information.

Annual Report, Central Bank of Ceylon, various issues.

Socio-economic Survey 1973 and *Socio-economic Survey 1980* (Colombo: Central Bank of Ceylon, 1974 and 1981).

HOLLIS CHENERY *et al.*, *Redistribution with Growth* (Oxford: Oxford University Press, 1974).

Sri Lanka: an Emerging Business Centre (London: Economist Intelligence Unit, 1980).

D.M. FORREST, *A Hundred Years of Ceylon Tea, 1867-1967* (London: Chatto & Windus, 1968).

ARNOLD C. HARBERGER (ed.), *World Economic Growth* (San Francisco: Institute for Contemporary Studies, 1984).

H.N.S. KARUNATILLEKE, *Economic Development in Sri Lanka* (New York: Praeger, 1971).

W.A. LEWIS, *Growth and Fluctuations: 1870-1913* (London: Allen & Unwin, 1978).

THEODORE MORGAN and NYLE SPOCLESHA (eds), *Economic Interdependence in South Asia* (Madison: University of

Wisconsin Press, 1969).

DONALD R. SNODGRASS, *Ceylon: an Export Economy in Transition* (Homewood, Illinois: Richard D. Irvin, 1966).

SYDNEY J. WELLS, *International Economics* (London: Allen & Unwin, 1969).

A.J. WILSON, in K.M. DeSilva (ed.), *Sri Lanka Survey* (London: Hurst, 1977.)

Studies on Participation in the GATT System

AS PART of the Trade Policy Research Centre's programme of studies on the Participation of Developing Countries in the International Trading System, three general studies have been published, focussing on economic and legal issues in the GATT system *per se*.

Myths and Reality of External Constraints on Development, by James Riedel, of Johns Hopkins University's School of Advanced International Studies in Washington, questions the widely-held belief that conditions in developed countries determine the growth of exports from, and the availability of capital to, developing countries. To free themselves from this perceived 'external constraint', many developing countries have insisted on the need to pursue industrialization through import-substitution policies, on their need to borrow on concessional terms and on their need to be accorded preferential access to developed-country markets.

Professor Riedel argues that there is now a genuine alternative to these policies and demands for special privileges. With developing countries diversifying their exports and moving into the production of industrial products, they can now seek more secure access to the markets of developed countries, provided that they can retain their competitiveness. Similarly, he examines the implications of developing countries receiving improved access to capital markets, particularly the opportunities this development makes. Much depends though on their own domestic policies in promoting economic development.

Economic Impact of Generalized Tariff Preferences, by Rolf J. Langhammer, a Senior Research Fellow at the Institut für Weltwirtschaft, Kiel, and André Sapir, Professor of Economics at the Free University of Brussels, analyzes the effects of the schemes under the Generalized System of Preferences (GSP) that are operated by the European Community and the United States. The GSP is a formal derogation from the principle of non-discrimination, the cornerstone of the GATT. Developing countries have contested the principle of non-discrimination and the GSP has come to symbolize their demands for 'special and more favourable treatment' of their exports of manufactures and semi-manufactures to developed countries.

There is little evidence, the authors conclude, that preferences are effective in stimulating developing-country exports. Indeed, the way those preferences are administered reflects an overall protectionist tendency in developed-country trade policies, especially discrimination against successful developing-country exporters.

Developing countries need to focus on the liberalization of non-tariff measures and on general tariff liberalization. The more advanced, in particular, would be better advised to participate in the reciprocal bargaining process of the Uruguay Round negotiations now proceeding in Geneva rather than insist on their continued eligibility for tariff preferences.

Developing Countries in the GATT Legal System, by Robert E. Hudec, Steen Professor of Law at the University of Minnesota, traces the evolution of the GATT's current legal policy towards developing countries, detailing the successive departures from GATT obligations to satisfy demands for 'special and differential treatment'. In a growing conflict over the role developing countries should play in the international trading system, developed countries are calling on developing countries to assume fuller participation in legal disciplines of the GATT. Professor Hudec questions the assumption that fuller legal participation by developing countries will bring about greater access to developed-country markets, but it will enable developing countries to achieve better internal control over their own trade policies, he argues.

The study concludes that the GATT's current legal policy has failed to serve the interests of its developing-country members and ends by proposing several policy initiatives to begin the long and difficult task of reversing that policy.

List of Thames Essays

OCCASIONAL papers of the Trade Policy Research Centre are published under the omnibus heading of Thames Essays. Set out below are the particulars of those published to date. The first 44 titles were published under the Centre's sole imprint, but they may also be obtained from the Gower Publishing Company, its address in the United Kingdom, the United States of America and Australia being set out in the reverse of the title page of this essay.